PORK BARREL

PORK BARREL

The Unexpurgated
Grace Commission Story
of Congressional Profligacy

RANDALL·FITZGERALD AND GERALD LIPSON

CATO
INSTITUTE

Library of Congress Cataloging in Publication Data

Fitzgerald, Randall.
  Porkbarrel: the unexpurgated Grace Commission
  story of congressional profligacy.

  1. Administrative agencies—United States.
2. United States—Executive departments. 3. United
States. Congress. 4. Waste in government
spending—United States. 5. President's Private
Sector Survey on Cost Control (U.S.) I. Lipson,
Gerald, 1935–   II. Title.

JK585.F58   1984   353.04   84-21493
ISBN 0-932790-44-5

Printed in the United States of America.

This report was originally prepared under the title "The
Cost of Congressional Encroachment."

CATO INSTITUTE
224 Second Street SE
Washington, D.C. 20003

Contents

Foreword

Eugene J. McCarthy

This report is in some cases oversimplified; undoubtedly some things are not in full context. Extenuating circumstances, in some instances, have gone unrecognized and unreported. Despite the report's focus on congressional profligacy, it gives members of Congress, especially those named in the report, grounds for protesting that executive and bureaucratic profligacy is as bad as their own, if not worse. However, taken as a whole, the report is not only defensible but also commendable. Its authors and publishers deserve special credit for providing names of members of Congress primarily responsible for particularly wasteful and self-interested expenditures, and especially for noting that some of the persons so named have built or sought to build reputations as guardians of the public purse. The authors suggest that the reputation of some of the economizers is a "Never on Sunday" reputation and applies only to expenditures for projects and programs outside the member's own district or state.

Some members of Congress clearly employ a double standard regarding projects of questionable economic justification—one standard for application at home, and another for the rest of the country. Their political opponents, the state or local press, and even the local Chamber of Commerce are likely to exhibit the same inconsistency by declaring their own commitments to frugality and austerity, in general, but denouncing incumbents for failing to protect or advance special interests of the state or district.

The book also deals successfully with wastefulness in the context of historical and traditional practices, and with the institutional and, in some cases, statutory encouragement of waste. The classic and clearest demonstration of the interworking of traditional, institutional, and personal political interests is found in the portion of the book dealing with water policy and projects. Members of Congress like to give their constituency tangible evidence of the effectiveness of their representation: a new Post Office, a veterans' hospital, a government office building, a government contract, a road, a bridge.

But no project seems to be as intensely sought after as a water project. Even though a congressional rule states that no project can be named after a living politician, there is always the possibility that such a project can later be renamed and live on in history as a dam, lock, or canal carrying the name of a deceased member of Congress, or perhaps one who is retired and has passed the biblically allotted three score years and ten. Such temptations all too often are too much for austerity-minded members to bear, and their judgment is all too frequently fogged by the illusion of immortality thus obtained.

Congressional power over water projects began with the authorization of the first Rivers and Harbors Act in 1824. That power, although shared minimally with the executive branch, has been assiduously guarded by Congress. President Carter, a stranger to Washington, discovered this soon after his inauguration when he announced his intention to eliminate some 18 water projects from the Public Works Appropriation Bill. One of the projects was the Central Arizona Project. I was in Arizona at the time of the announcement and noted that despite the president's statement, the bulldozers and other earth-moving equipment continued to operate as if no presidential announcement had been made. The workers either had not heard of the president's opposition or had ignored it. In either case, they were right: The project continued.

Another voice bearing on the success of Congress in pushing water projects is that of the Army Corps of Engineers, which over the years has established a mutually beneficial relationship with Congress. The corps has aided Congress in obtaining approval of projects, and in turn has been assisted in its need for continuous work in lowering mountains, raising valleys, deepening the rivers, drying up swamps, and generally making "straight the way of the Lord." It has been suggested that the corps be given responsibility for nuclear power plant construction, supervision, and waste disposal (if that be possible), so as to give it something to do, and thereby distract it from water or land projects. Few members of Congress, however, would want to have their names associated with a nuclear waste dump.

Running a close second to water projects in congressional popularity are, as the book indicates, military installations of every kind, even testing grounds, though these are less popular. Congressman Quentin Burdick of North Dakota expressed the general attitude of members of Congress when he responded to an administration spokesman's announcement of intention to move a military installation to another site. The spokesman listed all the advantage of closing the North Dakota operation, including how he thought the congressman's constituents would be pleased to learn of the economies that would result from the shutdown. The congressman responded with an anecdote about the famous Sioux Indian chief, Sitting Bull: In the terms of his surrender to the U.S. Government, Sitting Bull had agreed to live by the white man's law, but was found to have two wives. On being brought to court and told by the judge that he could keep only one wife, the chief filled his pipe and smoked it until all the tobacco was gone. He then nodded to the judge, indicating that he accepted the rule. The judge then advised the chief to return to the reservation and tell the wife he was giving up to move to another house. The chief again filled his pipe, smoked it, and then, when all the tobacco was gone, said to the judge, "You go tell her." So said Burdick to the administration spokesman, "You go tell them."

Besides traditional Porkbarrel projects, there are some programs that, once started, simply "grow." Fitzgerald and Lipson appropriately take note of these, especially as demonstrated by commissaries, established to serve the needs of service persons and other government employees who were denied access to necessary or desirable consumer goods. Begun with good intentions and to serve a defined need, the commissaries have become a consumer service, now running a close second to Sears, Roebuck and operating in metropolitan areas where every reasonable consumer need can be satisfied through private-sector retail or wholesale stores. Other such programs include those to give financial aid to impacted areas (areas of the country affected by government installations) and the bilingual education program.

Certain also to receive vigorous, even heroic, support from members of Congress are small rural post offices in sparsely populated regions. Senator Harry Byrd of Virginia, a fiscal conservative and sincere advocate of economy in government, drew the line on these offices. They were, he held, necessary not only to handle the mail, but also as centers for public assembly, reminders of national loyalty and of patriotic duty.

Projects and installations of limited and regional interest also stir strong protective instincts that easily override the considerations of economy in government. This report provides good examples of how such instincts have saved fish hatcheries and weather stations, especially if the weather station is in tornado country. Congressional concern is understandable in the latter case because with a weather station closed, the congressman is not likely to be blamed for the tornado itself, but may well be blamed for the consequences.

If the book is to be faulted (and almost any book can be faulted on this point), it is that it does not go far enough in covering the whole range of government waste and profligacy, particularly the contribution of the executive branch to fiscal irresponsiblity. Like Congress, the executive branch has its own agenda of porkbarrel projects. But the executive branch is often involved in matters of greater sweep, with much larger sums of money at stake. And Congress usually concurs in these acts. The increase in Social Security payments adopted in 1972, involving billions of dollars, is a clear example. As the November 1972 election approached, an increase in Social Security payments was, according to tradition, expected. President Nixon announced that he wanted a 5 percent increase and that he would veto any increase above that. The Democratic Congress was not to be beaten. The Democratic leaders reportedly considered a 10 percent increase, but were so suspicious of Nixon that they believed that instead of vetoing the increase, he would take credit for it with the electorate. In any case, Congress raised Social Security payments by 20 percent and provided that the increase go into effect in October 1972, just before the November elections. One assumes that they thought that a president who had said he would veto any increase above 5 percent would surely veto a 20 percent increase, if it were called to his attention. Nixon not only did not veto the increase, but the October Social Security checks included a note advising the recipients of the 20 percent increase, and also advising them that Richard Nixon had signed the bill.

In that same pre-election period, President Nixon announced an increase in the dairy price support, saying that he was merely heading off a congressional move to increase the support price. He was probably right. In somewhat the same spirit, President Reagan announced that even though the formula for increasing Social Security payments on the basis of inflation would not require an increase this year, he is going to recommend an increase anyway. He probably anticipated a similar move by Congress, which may well be waiting for him to set the measure of increase he wants before proposing a greater increase. Thus while Common Cause and other reformers deplore the millions spent on presidential and congressional campaigns and other groups oppose the federal financing of campaigns, billions of dollars will be paid out quite directly from the federal treasury, and credit for the payments will be claimed by both the president and members of Congress.

Defense procurement is another field of happy spending by the executive and legislative branches. Especially as presidential elections approach, we can expect a flood of announcements of contract awards and other allocations of funds. NASA plans one more shuttle flight before the November 1984 elections. If hard pressed politically, Reagan might be moved to substitute his vice president for the school teacher he has announced will soon be put in orbit. And there will undoubtedly be more exhibitions of the B-1 bomber in its alphabetical variations of B-1-A or B-1-B, as it moves through its nine lives. One member of Congress said that although he had voted for weapons and weapons systems that were obsolete before completed, the request for his support of the B-1 was the first time he had been asked to vote for an instrument of war that was obsolete even before production had started.

A recent newspaper story about the B-1 reports that manufacturers and scientific researchers in over 40 states are supplying materials, engineering, or equipment for the bomber. It should have wide popular support in Congress and be good for the economy at least in the short run, even though there is grave doubt that it will do much to increase the national security.

In that respect the B-1 is hardly unique in our history. In the 1920s the role of the cavalry in our military establishment was being reduced, and as a consequence there were reductions in the numbers of cavalry men, horses, and posts. The closing of Fort Snelling in Minnesota was the cause of serious objections on a variety of grounds: national security, local and regional economic impact, especially on saddle and harness makers, horse breeders, and hay and oats producers.

Fort Snelling and the B-1 are symbolic of the general problem addressed in this book: The political system causes members of Congress to defend their own constituents'—or contributors'—interests even when they know that those parochial interests conflict with the national interest. Fitzgerald and Lipson have done the country a service in exposing and detailing Congress's expensive porkbarrel habits. The book serves as a warning of just how pervasive and dangerous this habit is, and it should serve to alert taxpayers and voters of what really goes on behind the scenes while members of Congress make pious speeches about deficit reduction and fiscal responsibility.

Preface

At the head of the long conference table sat the Department of Energy's assistant secretary for administration, William Heffelfinger. His thick fingers drummed rapidly on a 6-inch pile of the agency's appropriations reports, its pages festooned with paperclips. To Heffelfinger's right sat his chief assistant, Harry Peebles, and two young career staffers from the Budget and Congressional Liaison offices. A large, rotund political appointee in his late fifties, Heffelfinger nudged his glasses up the bridge of his nose, smiled benignly at his two visitors, and asked, for the second time, "What can we do for you?"

We glanced at each other with upraised eyebrows, for the question made no sense. We had called Heffelfinger several days before to explain what we wanted and to request an interview. He had said he needed a few days to gather the information we sought— the information we assumed was contained in those paperclipped reports. Now he was feigning ignorance of his previous conversation with us.

Shrugging this aside, we again explained our mission. The President's Private Sector Survey on Cost Control, otherwise known as the Grace commission, after its chairman, New York business tycoon J. Peter Grace, had been established by President Reagan in June, 1982, to conduct a comprehensive study of the Executive Branch of the federal government with an eye to identifying—and hopefully eliminating—wasteful spending. The survey was being conducted by teams of executives from the business world, who served at no cost to the government.

As the teams delved into the operations of the federal government, they discovered more and more instances where program decisions were made not by federal officials who signed the papers, but by Congress, through the legislative and appropriations process.

As the magnitude of these instances became apparent, Peter Grace and his immediate associates concluded that much of the responsibility for excessive spending lay not with the government but with Congress.

Thus it was that we were engaged to research and write a report to the president examining how Congress has raised the cost of the federal government through pork-barreling and micromanagement of internal Executive agency affairs. We were interviewing top officials of the twenty largest cabinet departments and independent agencies. We were seeking only information that could be fully documented from the public record, and we were not interested in policy questions. We wanted names and examples of instances in which members of Congress had forced the agencies to spend funds on activities the agencies considered useless or wasteful, or in which Congress had intervened to prevent the agencies from instituting improvements in management and operational efficiency. We did not care who supported or opposed the MX missile, or whether the Central Intelligence Agency should support the Contras in Nicaragua; nor were we concerned about the party affiliation of those singled out for mention in our report.

The smile that had played faintly over Heffelfinger's face broke into a wide bureaucratic grin. He spread his arms expansively, drawing attention to his ample girth, and began regaling us with anecdotes that were interesting but largely irrelevant. He talked about the size of his agency and the diversity of its responsibilities. "What you are looking for—a lot of that goes on." But the problem, he insisted, was to define what constituted "pork" and micromanagement and then to separate that from policy matters. "It's a very difficult and complex thing to do," Heffelfinger cautioned, "and you must understand our situation."

His "situation" was a long-running feud with Rep. John Dingell (D–Mich.), chairman of the House Committee on Energy and Commerce, with jurisdiction over the Department of Energy. "Why, that man once tried to have me indicted," Heffelfinger exclaimed, motioning back over his shoulder in the direction of Capitol Hill. When Heffelfinger was first appointed director of administration for Energy in 1977, during the Carter administration, Dingell had raised questions about his suitability for office. Heffelfinger had previously been fired from the Department of Transportation, where he had served during both the Nixon and Ford administrations, following accusations that he was a "Republican hatchet man" on political appointments.

Now, Heffelfinger insisted, he would do nothing more that might antagonize Dingell and the Energy committee. "He'd drag my hind-end up before that committee of his," Heffelfinger predicted, flailing his arms about. "Long after your report is gone and forgotten, we'll still have to live with those people up on the Hill."

Though disappointed, and somewhat puzzled, we were not totally surprised by his reaction. Already officials of two other agencies—the Veterans Administration and the Environmental Protection Agency—had refused outright to meet us, citing fears of congressional retaliation. A third agency, the Department of Defense, had declined to help us identify costly and unnecessary military bases and commissaries, or to state which members of Congress were instrumental in keeping them open despite the spending burdens imposed. In several other agencies, which we prefer not to identify, officials provided sub-rosa cooperation. They would not meet us in person; our questions and their answers were shuttled back and forth on unmarked stationery, sometimes in unmarked envelopes, hand carried by messengers to avoid alerting bureaucrats who might inform friends on Capitol Hill that the agency was identifying big-spending, micromanaging lawmakers.

The meeting with Heffelfinger and his aides broke up and we concluded that we had run into another stone wall. As we filed out of the conference room, feeling rather frustrated by the entire encounter, Heffelfinger, in what seemed almost like an afterthought, invited us into his private office to see a framed award of merit he had received. As the two of us entered, Peebles, who had accompanied us, shut the door. The other two bureaucrats returned to their offices. Heffelfinger settled into a reclining leather chair behind his desk, and once more his fingers began tapping on the 6-inch stack of reports, which he had carried with him from the conference room. "Now," he said in a low but emphatic voice, "what can I do for you?"

Momentarily at a loss for words, one of us finally blurted out something to the effect that "we'd like your help in tracking down the boondoggles hidden in your budget."

"In that case," Heffelfinger replied, chuckling, "I can save you some time." He thrust at us the stack of pages culled from appropriations reports, saying, "We spent several days going through these after you called." Dozens of pages had been paperclipped, with relevant passages overlined in yellow.

In a confiding, solicitous tone, Heffelfinger proceeded to describe how energy technology and related project areas in the department's budget were replacing agriculture and public works projects as the new congressional pork on which the special interests with friends in Congress were feeding. "But I couldn't say that in front of those other two," he added, referring to the two younger career-ists who had sat at the conference table. "They would see it only in terms of their jobs being at stake."

We took the thick packet of papers from Heffelfinger, with the understanding that after studying them for a day or two, we would call him or Peebles if we had any questions. For the next several days we pored over the appropriations language he had collected. Our initial elation rapidly turned to bewilderment. The material was utterly incomprehensible to us. It described, in very technical terms, funding for everything from projects in high-energy physics to others concerned with development of esoteric synthetic fuels. One had to be a combination of electrical engineer, chemist, and high-energy physicist to be able to understand the projects described. And hundreds of millions of dollars were involved. There was no way, especially with only the short period of time we had available, for us to separate the worthwhile projects from those that could be considered a waste of taxpayer funds.

When we sought Heffelfinger's guidance again, we were told he was "not available," but that his assistant, Harry Peebles, would interpret the material for us. After a 1-hour session with Peebles, it became clear what kind of game was being played. The key to our investigation was identifying spending requirements that had not been requested by the agency or that had been imposed on it by Congress over the agency's objections. Example after example was dismissed by Peebles as not falling within those guidelines. As for other examples, he said the agency experts most familiar with them were not available. In the middle of this hour-long session, Peebles took a phone call and, after hanging up, announced that he had to go to the Middle East for an international oil conference in the next day or so—and would be extremely unavailable as a result.

We had been treated to a quadruple whammy. First, in the initial phone call, Heffelfinger had indicated he not only was aware of our mission but was prepared to be as helpful as possible. Second, in a meeting that included two career bureaucrats, whose reason for being there was never made clear, Heffelfinger and Peebles elabo-rately disavowed our entire project. Third, as that meeting broke up, we were invited into a private session where, once again, full cooperation and assistance was guaranteed. Fourth, when it came down to actually pinpointing specific examples, and interpreting them in the appropriations reports, nothing was delivered.

We describe this incident in such detail because it illustrates so well the real power relationships in the federal city. Heffelfinger is considered to be among the most effective and shrewd "nonbureaucratic" civil servants in the city. He is a classic survivor, respected by leaders of both Democratic and Republican administrations, which have retained him in service. The charade he went through with us demonstrated his nimble ability to dance between two adversarial power centers—an influential presidential commission on the one hand and a powerful member of Congress on the other—while appearing to cooperate with each against the other. Heffelfinger's performance demonstrates that the true conflicts over spending lie not just between the major parties, or even between conservatives and liberals, but between the executive branch and Congress.

Because of this conclusion that the conflicts over spending are more institutional than partisan or ideological, we have deliberately omitted party labels when identifying members of Congress.

All but a relative handful of the more than two million federal civil servants are careerists who entered the government through the competitive process, enjoy permanent status, and cannot be fired as presidential administrations change. The handful consists of a few thousand others, who are political appointees, such as cabinet secretaries, agency administrators, and their immediate assistants and associates, and who are named by the president to carry out, as best they can, the policies of his administration.

In most agencies control of daily program activities usually resides in the hands of careerists who have worked with those programs over the years. While the political appointees change with administrations, and sometimes more often, the careerists remain through the years, protecting their programs and (understandably) their jobs.

These careerists, almost all of them college graduates and many with advanced degrees, generally have not joined the federal government with the avowed aim of being shiftless and wasteful, wallowing in inefficiency, or determined to perform as little work as possible. Highly trained and generally dedicated, most of them would prefer to do as competent a job as they believe they are able, and to be recognized for it.

Unfortunately, unlike the private sector, with its profit and loss statements, the government has no objective method of measuring the efficiency of most programs. About the only analyses that matter are those of the leaders of the client groups and special interests that benefit from the programs, and those of key members of Congress. If they are pleased, a program thrives, but often their being pleased has little to do with how well the intended job is being performed or at what cost to the taxpayers.

So, very early in their budding careers, the ambitious civil servants learn that keeping important members of Congress and their political constituencies happy is far more important to their own future prospects than helping outside investigators to identify waste and mismanagement.

Not surprisingly most of the administration officials who cooperated in our study were political appointees with no stake in a career under future administrations. They could freely follow a commitment to reducing unnecessary waste. In addition a few career professionals, prompted by a sense of propriety, did brave the wrath of Congress and their fellow bureaucrats to help us, all under the strictest assurances of anonymity; but they were the exceptions.

Even so, in the short time available for this study, we were able to accumulate well over a hundred examples of pork-barreling and micromanagement from officials of the seventeen federal agencies we surveyed. The members of Congress responsible for this excess spending were almost evenly divided between Democrats and Republicans, and liberals and conservatives, thereby demonstrating that the appetite for spending respects no ideological or partisan bounds and that the problem of restraining spending is an institutional problem.

We devised a term to describe this congressional compulsion, calling it the parochial imperative. We defined it as an excessive preoccupation with the local impact of spending decisions at the expense of the national interest, especially the twin goals of a balanced federal budget and reduced levels of spending. This parochial imperative is exercised by members of Congress in at least five ways:

1. Bringing new federal spending into a state or district for projects of dubious value or necessity (the traditional pork barrel).
2. Legislatively enacting subsidies benefiting narrow economic or social interests in a state or district.
3. Circumventing competitive bidding procedures designed to

ensure that government services are provided at the lowest possible cost.

4. Canceling liabilities of state and local governments to the federal government.
5. Preventing changes or reductions in the size and structure of the federal government by legislating personnel requirements in the agencies and by vetoing reorganization plans that affect federal facilities at the local level.

One illustration of the parochial imperative in action occurred in June 1984, after our report was released. During consideration of an $18 billion water projects bill authorizing new dams, canals, and bridges in hundreds of congressional districts, the House of Representatives barely defeated (204 to 201) an attempt to deauthorize a $500 million canal across Florida that had first been proposed 42 years earlier as a haven from Nazi U-boats. The principal supporter of the canal, octogenarian Rep. Claude D. Pepper, who had steered the original bill for the 110-mile waterway through Congress in 1942, won the vote despite opposition from most other Florida state and federal lawmakers.

Rep. Pepper prevailed because most members of Congress adhere to a principle known as the "pork-barrel ethic," which means that members are expected to vote for colleagues' pet projects, regardless of merit, and then receive similar favors in return. When cost-conscious House members mutinied against this "ethic" and nearly defeated Rep. Pepper's canal, Rep. James J. Howard of New Jersey, chairman of the Public Works and Transportation Committee, circulated a list of members' names with black spots next to those whose own projects would be killed if they voted against any of the other water projects in the bill. This blackmail apparently worked, as each of the projects was approved, and even an attempt to force state and local governments to pay a larger share of the cost of federal water projects was soundly defeated, 213 to 85.

Two members of Congress were mentioned most frequently in our agency survey as perpetrators of the parochial imperative— Rep. Jamie L. Whitten of Mississippi and Sen. James A. McClure of Idaho. Both are influential committee chairmen—Whitten of the House Appropriations Committee and McClure of the Senate Energy and Natural Resources Committee—and both have been described, at one time or another, as "fiscal conservatives."

From preserving federal fish hatcheries, to securing bailouts for cotton farmers, to widening highways in his district, Whitten has not hesitated to use his chairmanship for the folks back home regardless of either the example he sets for his colleagues or the impact his actions have on the federal budget. Whitten justifies his attitude this way: "If you help a district, you are helping the nation. What happens in the district happens in the country." It is an attitude that, once adopted by each member of Congress, would be used, in the absence of self-restraint, to justify every spending scheme ever conceived.

Sen. McClure has masterminded legislation that prevents the executive branch from even studying the reduction of taxpayer subsidies for cheap energy to Northwestern states. He has used his chairmanship to prevent the federal government from selling $2 billion in excess silver to narrow the budget deficit because the sale would lower prices for the mining industry of his state. He has kept a federal subsidy to mining scholarships in place even though there is no demand for new mining engineers. He has continued the funding of subsidies for right-of-way costs on federal lands even though the prime beneficiaries are large oil companies such as Exxon. Somewhat more puzzling, McClure has shown a curiously excessive concern for the fiscal well-being of the American trust territories of Samoa and the Virgin Islands, consistently increasing their budgets beyond administration requests while ignoring reports of financial irregularities that cost millions in added taxpayer subsidies.

Other members of Congress singled out for frequent mention by agency officials included Senate minority leader Robert C. Byrd of West Virginia, Senate majority whip Ted Stevens of Alaska, Sen. Dennis DeConcini of Arizona, Sen. Charles H. Percy of Illinois, House speaker Thomas P. ("Tip") O'Neill, Jr. and Rep. Silvio O. Conte, both of Massachusetts, and Rep. Marvin Leath of Texas.

None of these or other lawmakers identified for our study, as well as none of the specific spending projects involved, were named in the final report when it was released to President Reagan on January 16, 1984. All such identification was deleted. As *Newsweek* magazine reported in its January 16 issue, commission chairman J. Peter Grace "apparently had caved in to the play-it-safe faction of his committee. Members of this group opposed release of the report at all on the grounds that it would skewer the very people whose support the commission needs to achieve its overall cost-cutting goals."

With more than 40 separate reports proposing nearly 2,500 recommendations for reform that promised to yield over $400 billion in savings over three years, the Grace commission felt it simply could not afford to alienate Congress when at least 70 percent of those recommendations required congressional approval for implementation and (as this report now shows) even the other 30 percent could be prevented or inhibited by Congress if it chose to do so. The members of the commission understood the institutional relationships as clearly as did William Heffelfinger.

Unfortunately J. Peter Grace found himself in a quandary. He had promised to name those who were perpetuating and exacerbating the problems his commission had identified. Grace had even been pictured on the cover of *U.S. News & World Report* describing Washington as "A City Without Guts."

As the principal authors of that "censored" report, we decided to resolve the quandary. While other employees of the commission had signed secrecy agreements pledging silence concerning what they learned about the federal agencies studied, we had not done so. On accepting our assignment with the commission, we had been assured that after our responsibilities to the commission were completed, we would be free to turn the report we produced, and anything else we learned, into magazine articles or a book. When the report was sanitized prior to release, we decided to exercise that option. This book is based upon an initial draft of the PPSSCC report with the names included.

We want to express our appreciation to Lisa Berger and Janice Sokil for their untiring research efforts; to counsel R. Stanley Harsh, who researched the item veto, and, especially to J. Peter Grace and the commission's chief operating officer, J. P. Bolduc, who supported and encouraged both the conception and implementation of the initial project.

Executive Summary

On June 30, 1982, President Reagan signed Executive Order 12369, which formally established the President's Private Sector Survey on Cost Control (PPSSCC), in the executive branch of the federal government under the chairmanship of J. Peter Grace. It quickly became known popularly as the "Grace Commission." An executive committee was established, consisting of 161 high-level private-sector executives—mostly chairmen and chief executive officers—from many of the nation's leading corporations.

Briefly stated, the president directed the PPSSCC to:

- Identify opportunities for increased efficiency and reduced costs achievable by executive action or legislation.
- Determine areas where managerial accountability can be enhanced and administrative controls improved.
- Suggest short- and long-term managerial operating improvements.
- Specify areas where further study can be justified by potential savings.
- Provide information and data relating to governmental expenditures, indebtedness, and personnel management.

The executive order also provided that "the Committee is to be funded, staffed and equipped . . . by the private sector without cost to the Federal Government." To implement this objective, the Foundation for the President's Private Sector Survey on Cost Control was established. It formed a survey management office, which organized so-called task forces, each of which was to be cochaired by two or more members of the executive committee.

The management office assigned twenty-two of these task forces to study specific departments and agencies, and the remaining fourteen task forces to study certain functions, such as personnel, data processing, and procurement, on a governmentwide basis. In addition to individual task force reports, the management office scheduled a series of reports on selected issues. Apart from the cochairpersons, no task force member was also a member of the executive committee, and no task force had any authority to make recommendations to departments and agencies or to the president. That authority was vested in the PPSSCC executive committee.

Unlike most other PPSSCC reports, this report—one of those on selected issues—provides no estimate of cost savings that could be achieved through implementation of stated recommendations. The recommendations in this report are focused on identifying specific opportunities where relationships between the executive and legislative branches of government can be improved and the overall cost of government reduced.

Our objective in this special study was not to examine and evaluate the operations of Congress. Rather, our mandate was to study and evaluate operations of the executive branch to identify opportunities where improved efficiencies and resulting cost savings could be realized. Through this survey, and by reviewing the other task force reports, numerous instances were found in which the legislative branch had thwarted or impeded the operating efficiency of the executive branch. PPSSCC has therefore sought to establish how and why this occurred. The inquiry led PPSSCC to single out committees and members of Congress who had participated in certain actions found to perpetuate those inefficiencies.

The examples described in this report should not be interpreted as cause for embarrassment on the part of any committee or member of Congress, party, or ideology. Nor is any criticism intended to point to a conclusion that the powers of the legislative branch should be diminished or those of the executive branch increased. It should be noted that the PPSSCC recommendations contained in the initial report and incorporated in this report were not formulated with this or any administration or Congress in mind. The suggestions advanced are intended to help the executive and legislative branches achieve an optimum relationship in their efforts to improve governmental operations and reduce costs, regardless of the incumbent in the White House or the party makeup in Congress.

PPSSCC recognizes the risks inherent in the release of this report. It cites dozens of examples of Congress having impeded the efforts of the executive branch to achieve efficiencies and cost savings; yet the support and commitment of this same Congress is necessary to bring about the implementation of most PPSSCC recommendations.

Nonetheless PPSSCC believes that these issues must be reported, discussed, and addressed, and that the executive and legislative branches will rise above individual concerns and institutional rivalries to unite in a common cause that will result in a more efficient, effective, and responsive government at less cost to the taxpayers.

The Rise of "Micromanagement"

The PPSSCC findings demonstrate that Congress has expanded the scope of its concern for executive branch activities to include the most minute details of operations. These range from dictating the size and style of agency wall calendars to overruling a Treasury Department decision on a mailbox address for payments of tobacco taxes, to requiring the assignment of an attorney to a government office in Stillwater, Okla.

Selected examples of congressional involvement in such day-to-day management decisions, which are documented in this report, represent up to $10 billion in unnecessary costs, not counting those resulting from the inefficiencies of operation that ensue. Given the limitations, in terms of time and resources, of this report, that estimate must be considered modest.

This compulsion by Congress to "micromanage" the executive branch has been accompanied by a corresponding tendency of Congress to overlook the rising costs of its own operations. Congress has directed executive branch agencies to maintain minimum levels of employment that are higher than agency managers say they need, and to place personnel in locations where agency managers say they are not needed. For example the Department of Education wanted to reduce and consolidate its staff of collectors working on student loans, for an estimated savings of $5 million annually. Congress, however, directed the agency to make no changes in the size or location of that staff. Meanwhile, from 1973 to 1983 the congressional staff grew by 40 percent, from 14,609 to 20,458, while the total legislative branch budget more than doubled, from $645 million to $1.3 billion, a 102 percent increase.

Making Exceptions to Its Own Rules

Violating the principles of sound management, Congress has bent the rules it has written to make exceptions that these rules were designed to prevent. In the process, Congress has increased the costs of agency operations and in turn the costs to U.S. taxpayers. For example PPSSCC has identified instances where

- Congress has canceled state and local obligations to the federal government, thereby shifting the financial burden to the executive branch.
- Congress has established competitive requirements for grant programs, and then has set them aside to direct that grants totaling $52 million be awarded to local interests.
- Congress has circumvented the competitive system for contracts to the private sector and also bent safeguards surrounding the nation's strategic metals stockpile to serve parochial economic interests, at overall costs above $2 billion.

When the executive branch has proposed a macro, or national, approach to improving inefficient or ineffective operations—such as water resources policy or military base realignment—Congress frequently has responded to parochial rather than national interests. As a result costly and questionable water projects are still being funded, and outmoded, unnecessary military bases remain in operation at annual costs in excess of $2 billion.

Protecting the Status Quo

The results of this PPSSCC report also have demonstrated that Congress all too frequently assumes the role of protector of government employees at the expense of both efficient and effective executive branch operations and the interests of the taxpayers. Consider what happened when the Government Printing Office wanted to close or consolidate regional bookstores, many of them hidden from the public on the upper floors of large federal office buildings; when the Department of Defense proposed making commissaries self-sustaining; and when the Department of Housing and Urban Development wanted to move a regional office from Topeka, Kans., to Kansas City, Mo. In each instance Congress intervened and prevented the implementation of these executive branch actions.

Congress also has demonstrated a compulsion to resist private-sector involvement in operations run by the government, even when it has been shown by the executive branch that the private sector can perform those activities more efficiently and at less cost. This apparent public-sector bias in Congress extends beyond contracting out to the private sector and a suspicion of the business community. It is symptomatic of a deeper and more pervasive attitude—that the status quo of government, in its size, structure, and personnel, should be preserved regardless of the cost to the taxpayers.

A Litany of Examples

This limited study uncovered over 100 examples of Congress raising costs to the executive branch agencies and impeding efficient management. Here are eight representative examples of this meddling:

1. Congress refuses to allow the executive branch to even review the pricing structure of the Federal Power Marketing Administrations, which received over $250 million in taxpayer subsidies in FY 1984.
2. The Veterans Administration, with over 200,000 employees, must obtain congressional approval for any reorganization affecting as few as three employees.
3. A Senate committee chairman directs the appropriation of $7.1 million to paper over financial irregularities in American Samoa.
4. A House committee chairman obtains special legislation that delays the Department of Health and Human Services from recouping $354,000 that had been criminally misspent.
5. Civilian workers at an Air National Guard base are exempted from a governmentwide pay raise ceiling in order to receive a 27 percent pay increase through special-interest legislation.
6. A high-ranking senator exempts his state from the governmentwide competitive rate structure for moving the household goods of military families, an action that cost taxpayers at least $78 million from its inception in FY 1979 through FY 1983.
7. A Senate committee chairman prevents the sale of $2 billion worth of excess silver from the National Defense Stockpile and in the process benefits parochial interests.
8. A Senate committee, in a dispute with the House, refuses to approve requests for needed repairs on federal buildings that the General Services Administration must submit to Congress, adding a projected cost to taxpayers of over $150 million since FY 1979.

Abdicating Responsibility

Congress has conditioned itself generally to select the easiest and most politically expedient options. Naysayers, such as renowned Rep. H. R. Gross of Iowa, who gauge all congressional actions for their spending impact on taxpayers, are today an exceptional and rare breed. During an appearance of PPSSCC members before the

House Budget Committee on October 4, 1983, Rep. Delbert L. Latta of Ohio made this revealing observation:

> I don't think there is any question that the members of Congress, as a body, know what the problems are. The question in my mind after 25 years down here is whether or not they have the fortitude to do anything about it. It is more politically expedient to vote to do something for "good old Joe" or for this faction or that faction, and get re-elected, than it is to do something for the country.

When the framers of our Constitution emerged from their final deliberations in Philadelphia's Carpenters' Hall, a woman approached Benjamin Franklin and asked him what kind of government had been established. "A Republic, Madame," he replied, "If you can keep it." Some 50 years later, a visiting European was said to remark that the American Republic would last only until the people realized they had the power to vote themselves funds from the public treasury. The result, he predicted, would lead to economic disaster and despotism.

The American people, through narrow, parochial, and special-interest pressure on Congress, have been voting themselves funds from the public treasury until today we have a federal budget in excess of $850 billion, an annual deficit approaching $200 billion, and public debt totaling over $1.3 trillion. Congress controls the federal purse strings, the Constitution is clear and exact on that. If Congress does not respond to the PPSSCC recommendations to end this spending spiral, then what? And, if not now, then when? Can we afford to wait and risk financial catastrophe?

It has been said that "to govern is to choose." Congress, by refusing to make choices that may be politically painful, is abdicating its role as a responsible part of the governing process. If Congress will not make the hard choices, someone else must.

Introduction

Joe and Jane Mainstreet live in Averagetown, U.S.A. In every respect they are a statistically average American family, with one child (a second on the way), two cars (only one is paid for), a $44,850 home mortgage, a $2,265 income tax liability for the coming year, and (although they don't realize it) a liability of $23,523 or more, which represents their family share of the $1.38 trillion federal debt, as calculated by the Office of Management and Budget (OMB).

They are being interviewed by a local representative of a national polling organization, which is conducting a poll of attitudes about Congress. Let's listen in on their conversation:

Interviewer:	What do you think of Congress?
Joe and Jane (in unison):	They're a bunch of big spenders!
Interviewer:	What do you think of your own Congressman?
Joe (Jane nods her head):	Oh him, well, he's a pretty good guy!
Interviewer:	And why is that?
Joe:	When the Air Force wanted to close the base outside town, he wouldn't let them! Same with the Amtrak train. They wanted to shut the line down, said it cost too much. But he pulled some strings to keep it here, 'cause this town would be nothing without it.
Jane:	And he got the feds to build us a new lake where we can take the kids and swim for free now! He gets things done for his district!
Interviewer:	What do you think of the tax rate?
Joe (Jane grimaces):	Way too high! We won't be able to send our kids to college if they go any higher!
Interviewer:	What do you think about government spending?
Joe and Jane (in unison):	Out of control! Those big spenders in Congress are going to bankrupt the country!

This fictional exchange bears more than a casual connection to reality. A public opinion poll conducted nationwide during the summer of 1983 found that 31 percent of those sampled disapproved of the way Congress was handling its job, while only 10 percent disapproved of the way their own congressional representatives were handling themselves in office. Those 21 percentage points of difference may reflect as well the same sort of schizophrenic problem many Americans experience when they attempt to assess the impact of spending decisions made in Washington.

On the one hand many taxpayers think Congress exhibits a reckless disregard for the public purse, enacting policies and programs with no concern for the taxpayer burdens imposed. On the other hand some taxpayers often judge the effectiveness of their own elected representatives based on how many federal dollars he or she succeeds in siphoning out of the governing process and into their state or district. Thus the litmus test of survival in politics all too often becomes how loudly elected officials rail against taxes, spending, and debt, and how actively and successfully they pursue the parochial rewards that flow from the exercise of power and influence.

Congress is 535 diverse human beings—100 in the Senate, 435 in the House—each with his or her own parochial concerns and legislative agenda. Congress is an institution with power divided among 59 committees and 259 subcommittees, employing more than 20,000 support personnel, and spending an estimated $733 million in 1983 simply to function as a deliberative body.

Congress is a national institution elected at the local level to formulate national policies and programs to be carried out by the president and the executive branch agencies. Congress makes policy, the executive branch executes that policy, and the judiciary interprets it. But the executive agencies have responsibility without real authority. They spend money, but only that appropriated by Congress and only for purposes Congress chooses and approves.

The cumulative impact of spending decisions, large and small, that emanate from parochial concerns levies a toll on more than just the public purse. The parochial imperative of Congress—an excessive concern for, and interest in, the local impact of federal activities—often prevents the executive branch from administering government in the most efficient and cost-effective way. The tendency of Congress to fine tune the machinery of government can interfere with the ability of the executive branch to manage itself.

These interactions all too often carry with them cost burdens to the present taxpayers and also to succeeding generations.

More than 70 percent of the PPSSCC recommendations require congressional approval, but getting legislation passed by Congress is not an easy task. The 97th Congress saw 13,236 bills introduced, yet only 473 were enacted into law, or less than 4 percent. Recent history also demonstrates instances of the executive branch proposing a macro or national plan as a solution to a domestic problem and Congress subjecting it to the merciless scrutiny of micro or parochial points of view.

Because congressional action and commitment are required to eliminate the escalation of costs and mismanagement in the executive agencies, we must ask ourselves to what extent does Congress share in the responsibility for the current condition of the federal government and in the implementation of opportunities for improvement identified by PPSSCC? While recognizing that Congress has a legitimate, and indeed vital, oversight role with regard to the executive agencies, we must ask to what degree has Congress become fixated on details at the expense of broader national objectives. And finally, concerning our system of government, we must ask how much longer these conditions of waste, excessive spending, and uncontrolled deficits can persist until the Joe and Jane Mainstreets of America—and their elected representatives—begin to exercise self-restraint.

The Constitution created a system of three separate but equal branches of the federal government. Many people would argue, though, that Congress is more equal than the others because of its control over spending. The president can offer a program, but he has no authority to require Congress to even consider it, let alone grant approval.

The relationship between the executive and the legislative branches may seem especially confusing for Joe and Jane Mainstreet because of two events that take place every January and February, the State of the Union message and the submission of the federal budget, respectively. It can be said that the president, as the only public official elected to represent all of the people, is especially charged with representing the overall national interest, as reflected in the federal budget. The locally elected members of Congress, however, often are faced with cross-pressures of having to balance the national interests with the interests, if not demands, of their own constituents. The potential for conflict is built into their jobs.

More than 86 million voters cast ballots in the 1980 presidential election, which meant that (even taking into account the electoral college system) the winner needed the support of more than 40 million of them to be elected. That total translates into an average of fewer than 200,000 votes cast per congressional district. As Rep. Les Aspin of Wisconsin once told the *Washington Post*, "I don't care what my district thinks . . . as long as 51 percent of it likes me."

There lies the root of the parochial imperative. It is the need to meet the demands and serve the interests of that 51 percent of the voters to whom, at an irreducible minimum, a member of Congress must look to the exclusion if necessary of all other considerations.

Pressures behind this imperative are reinforced by the way Congress organizes itself to conduct its legislative business. Each of the committees and subcommittees concentrates on a rather narrow set of governmental services or activities. The most powerful of course are those that control the purse strings—the Appropriations and the Ways and Means committees in the House and the Appropriations and Finance committees in the Senate.

Between 1973 and 1975 Congress adopted a number of "reform" measures that have led to expanding the size, scope, and cost of congressional staff while erecting new power fiefdoms within the legislative structure. Among these changes are requirements that each committee have at least four subcommittees, and that the (majority) members have the right to elect the chairmen of those bodies. The chairmen in turn have the exclusive right to consider all bills and oversee all executive branch programs within their jurisdictions, as well as the authority to hire staff and the funds to pay them.

Until these changes happened, committee chairmen not only appointed the subcommittee chairmen but often decided whether there would be any subcommittees, and, if so, how many would be created and what roles they would play. Each committee chairman also controlled the committee staff. Thus, if a committee member wanted to hold a hearing on a bill, the chairman's approval was usually needed, sometimes even to the extent of obtaining approval for the use of a committee hearing room.

With the new expansion of subcommittee powers in the 1970s has come an expansion of committee staff and budget. For instance the eighteen regular standing committees of the House went from a total of 918 staff members in 1973 to 1,937 in 1980, an increase of 111 percent. In the same period the committees' budgets went from

$14.65 million to $40.60 million, an increase of 177 percent. Overall the past decade has seen congressional staff (including employees working for individual members) grow 40 percent from 14,609 in 1973 to 20,458 in 1983, while the total legislative branch budget has more than doubled, from $645 million to $1.3 billion, an increase of 102 percent.

Rep. James M. Collins of Texas, who left office in 1982, labeled the period the "era of subcommittee government" as he sought unsuccessfully to cut back on such growth. Calling the result of this growth "lack of coordination and duplication of work," Collins said that committee staff members then earning up to $52,500 a year had to "justify those high priced jobs" by "continuously inventing new ways to spend the American tax dollars."

The fragmentation of legislative authority and responsibility into 259 narrow-focus subcommittees, combined with pressures on House members to respond to the parochial imperative, has given committee staffers sufficient powers and incentive to manipulate and micromanage executive branch operations. This form of meddling can lead to serious and costly management problems—and it has, as this report shows.

The executive branch of government is divided into 13 executive departments and 58 independent agencies. Within this framework our federal government is the world's largest super conglomerate, with an operating budget in FY 1983 of $850 billion. It employs over 2.8 million civilians, operates 348 hospitals with 120,738 beds, and runs the world's largest automated data processing system with 17,000 computers. It is also the world's largest "bank," with $764.6 billion in loans outstanding, equal to the combined portfolios of the nation's 70 largest banks. It owns and operates over 436,000 cars, trucks, buses, and other specialty vehicles—the largest civilian fleet in the world. It is the largest landlord and tenant, occupying an estimated 405,200 buildings nationwide that contain 2.6 billion square feet of space.

Overseeing this vast operation are the federal executive managers, employed because of their general leadership and managerial skills, and their special knowledge of and abilities in specific subject areas of government. In the exercise of their responsibilities, these managers develop a broad, and in some areas detailed, understanding of the day-to-day operations they oversee. In addition to developing an understanding of and appreciation for their agency's culture and work environment, they also become intimately familiar with its operating strategy, structure, systems, and people. They are supported in this role by an agency staff able to provide the most detailed information, analyses, or advice needed for decision making. Together they are clearly most knowledgeable and informed about their agency operations.

By contrast, members of Congress rarely if ever possess sufficient information on which to base sound decisions about minor day-to-day operational matters. They are simply not equipped. Nor do they have sufficient time and expertise, despite the sizable increases in congressional staff, for a dual role that involves both a policy function and an operational/managerial oversight function.

Some basic tenets of efficient, effective, and responsive management in the private sector have equal application to government for relations between Congress and the executive agencies. These tenets include the following:

- People who execute program responsibility should be told what to accomplish, not how to do the job.
- They should be provided with the tools and sufficient authority to accomplish this mission.
- They should generally be given the flexibility to employ as they see best the personnel and other resources allocated to them to accomplish their mission.
- While executive branch executives should be monitored to see if they are accomplishing the stated mission, they should not be saddled with an outside presence that tells them how to do their job and constantly meddles in even the smallest details of their operations.

PPSSCC members, from the vantage point of their corporate management experience, know only too well what dire consequences can result when these basic tenets of good management are violated.

This report focuses on four basic management functions that must be present and executed by the executive branch of government if efficiency and cost effectiveness of operations are to be attained. Specifically these functions center on

1. The Agency Strategy—determining what the agency is (in most cases previously determined by Congress), what it is expected to accomplish, where it is headed, and when it will get there.

2. The Agency Structure—establishing the structure necessary to accomplish and support the strategy, and defining appropriate functions, organizational roles and responsibilities, and related authorities and reporting relationships.
3. The Agency Systems—developing the management and technical systems necessary to support the structure and accomplish the mission, including related practices, methods, procedures, and controls.
4. The Agency People—allocating, evaluating, and motivating people resources based on knowledge, skills, and abilities necessary to operate the systems that support the structure to accomplish the mission.

The interaction of Congress and the executive agencies as it relates to these four basic management functions examined by PPSSCC shows serious conflicts resulting in waste, inefficiencies, and higher costs to the taxpayers. This special report examines the role of Congress in connection with the financial crisis of excessive federal spending and deficits. This study was conducted through a process of interviews and of reviewing and analyzing legislation, committee hearings, PPSSCC task force reports, and the public record. Although a large portion of the available congressional and other government documentation was reviewed, the surface has barely been scratched.

But despite time and resource limitations, representative examples of congressional actions exacerbating the conditions of federal inefficiency and waste have been identified. Furthermore, as this report demonstrates, there are institutional and organizational problems in Congress that severely restrict executive branch performance. These are beyond the scope of this report.

I. The Agency Strategy: How Congress Impedes Executive Branch Cost-Cutting Objectives

Too often Congress mires itself in the parochial, or myopic, concerns of its individual members at the expense of broader national goals and interests. This excessive preoccupation with local impact, which we call the parochial imperative, frequently prevents the executive branch from achieving cost savings and efficiencies that could be of benefit to taxpayers and our nation as a whole. Too often when the executive branch proposes a national strategy or plan to solve a systemic problem, Congress invokes the parochial imperative and micromanages the plan until it no longer represents a viable national solution.

When the Carter administration proposed a nationwide plan to reduce the costs of water projects, Congress subjected it to such rigorous parochial scrutiny that only miniscule savings were achieved. When, beginning in the 1960s, a succession of administrations attempted to enact a national strategy for closing inefficient and costly military bases, Congress resisted and eventually so hamstrung the executive branch with legislative restrictions that unneeded, budget-draining bases are still being operated in large numbers. When the Ford administration proposed a nationwide reevaluation of military commissaries to decrease the taxpayer subsidy, Congress refused to make any change in the status quo.

The cumulative impact of parochial-based decisions is an almost complete freeze on the size, structure, and management strategies of government. Congress has offered no broad cost-cutting solutions of its own, so it is the taxpayers who suffer the consequences.

National Water Policy: "Playing to the Parochial Imperative"

Forty miles south of Kansas City, Kans., the Hillsdale Dam rises 75 feet above the placid waters of Hillsdale Lake, which was created by the dam. On a pleasant sunny afternoon the waters are dotted with tiny triangles of white and crisscrossed by the curving wakes of sailboats, powerboats, and the boats of folks just out fishing.

Very likely Joe and Jane Mainstreet are out there, using one of the two free boat ramps to get their craft into the water. Nearby is a public visitor center. All in all this is a very nice place to spend a quiet holiday, and apparently free of charge.

Hillsdale Dam and Lake make up one of 3,422 water development and flood-control projects built or being built, at a total federal investment of over $36 billion, since Congress authorized the first Rivers and Harbors Act in 1824. Completed in 1982 at a cost of $61.2 million, nearly 5.5 times its original estimate of $9.4 million, the Hillsdale project today is a relatively small monument to one of the fiercest legislative battles Congress has fought to preserve its parochial interest at the expense of a national perspective.

The fight, which began barely a month after Jimmy Carter was inaugurated as president in 1977, continued for nearly two years and did not end until he had to exercise a veto. It is worth examining in detail because it illustrates, in rare fashion, the elements that make up the clash between parochial and national needs.

From the earliest days of the Republic, Congress has considered the development of water resources a special part of its own political domain. Congress traditionally has approved each decision to undertake such projects as a Hillsdale Dam and Lake, including its detailed specifications. And each year, through the annual public works appropriations bill (recently renamed the energy and water development appropriations bill), Congress doles out precise amounts of money for the planning, design, and construction of these projects. Because every project is precisely located, and thus precisely local, the interests of affected representatives and senators is always an integral part of this particular governing process. As a result each project is evaluated on a case-by-case basis, on its own merits. Through this perhaps not intended, much less planned for, piecemeal approach, Congress has formulated what in the end has become the nation's water resources policy.

In the course of his 1976 bid for the White House, then former governor Jimmy Carter campaigned as both a conservationist and a fiscal conservative. Among other things he pledged to halt the construction of unnecessary and environmentally destructive dams and to generally reform what then passed for national water resources programs. In essence he promised to put a lid on the pork barrel.

Well before inauguration day, a transition team was preparing to

2

redeem that pledge, reviewing a broad range of projects that had been included in the 1978 public works budget submitted to Congress by President Ford shortly before he left office.

Every newly elected president seeks to make his mark as soon as possible. The first opportunity usually comes by seeking revisions in the last federal budget submitted by an outgoing predecessor. There is a long overlap between the federal budget cycle and the beginning of each new presidential term of office. The federal fiscal year begins on October 1, but the president must by law submit his proposed budget for that fiscal year the preceding February, thus giving Congress eight months to consider the president's agenda in light of its own priorities.

Each presidential budget itself is the culmination of a process that runs for well over a year, beginning with estimates of spending requirements and proposals in executive agency offices that work their way through cabinet-level decisions to the Office of Management and Budget and ultimately to the president.

Thus, a newly elected president enters office with several years of his first (and perhaps only) administration already programmed by a predecessor. He takes office four months into a fiscal year that began a full month before the election he won. At the same time the budget for the fiscal year that will begin when the new administration is eight months in office already has been submitted to Congress, obviously reflecting the spending priorities of the preceding administration. About the only way a new president can begin to show immediate action on the budget is to propose changes in the one just submitted to Congress.

On February 22, 1977, President Carter announced his intention to reevaluate about 300 of the 506 water resource projects that were in President Ford's FY 1978 budget, with an eye to deleting those that no longer made economic or environmental sense. At the same time Carter named a number of projects for which he said he already was inclined to end funding. Many of the projects approved in the past "under different economic circumstances and at times of lower interest rates are of doubtful necessity now, in light of new economic conditions and environmental policies," he said.

Within a day of the president's statement, members of Congress were blistering him for attempting to "usurp" their traditional prerogatives. So began a running battle between the executive branch and Congress that, although it rose and dipped in intensity, did not end until the near close of the 95th Congress. Even members with national reputations as supporters of the environment and as budget cutters joined the chorus once it appeared their states or districts were affected.

Rep. Morris K. Udall of Arizona, chairman of the House Interior Committee and known as a strong environmentalist, took sharp issue with President Carter's questioning of the $1.3 billion Central Arizona Project, a massive and controversial undertaking to divert water from the Colorado River for use in central and lower Arizona. Calling the president's decision "very hasty," Udall said it was like "pronouncing a verdict of guilty before the trial."

Two other representatives with reputations as fiscal conservatives, Eldon Rudd of Arizona and Mickey Edwards of Oklahoma, said the cuts smacked of an "imperial Presidency." Within two days Interior Secretary Cecil Andrus was before Chairman Udall's committee insisting that "there have been no permanent decisions" as yet.

The fact that a $900 million dam in California would be sited in an earthquake zone, while a $436 million reclamation project in North Dakota was souring relations with Canada, did not deter members of Congress from those states from defending the projects and attacking the president for proposing to delete them from the budget.

The congressional heat was so intense that within days President Carter began to back away. On February 28, less than a week after the announcement, Florida Governor Reuben Askew, then chairman of the National Governors Conference, reported that the president had assured a group of Western governors that he was not prejudging disposition of any projects then under review.

Finally, on April 18, President Carter announced he would formally ask Congress to delete from the 1978 public works appropriations bill funding for 18 projects, for a saving of $177.4 million, or 1.7 percent of the 1978 budget of $10.2 billion proposed for energy and water development for the coming fiscal year. Total savings, should the projects be canceled entirely, would amount to $2.5 billion.

Charged with shaping the 1978 public works bill in the House was Tom Bevill, a six-term congressman from Alabama's fourth district, an area with a strong populist tradition. Bevill reflected the philosophy that government should spend liberally on public works and in the process provide public service jobs. He had just assumed chairmanship of the Public Works Appropriations Subcommittee,

4

and few expected him to begin his tenure by cutting projects willingly. Of the 18 cuts sought by President Carter, Bevill's subcommittee agreed to one, a project near Topeka, Kans., at a budgetary saving of $1 million for the year. The cut was considered so marginal that even the member in whose district the project was located declined to defend it.

So, as the 1978 public works bill headed for the House floor, the initial response by Congress to a request by the president for a $177.4 million spending cut was to give him $1 million of it. With signals flying that Congress was not going to cooperate on the water projects issue, the first hints of a presidential veto began to be heard. A veto is the ultimate legislative weapon that a president has against the Congress. It takes two-thirds of those present and voting in both legislative bodies to override a veto.

A veto may sound like a strong threat, but the pressure of practical politics requires a president to weigh its use very carefully. For one thing a veto is all or nothing, involving the entire measure sent to the president for his signature. Unlike the governors of 43 states who have authority to veto specific items in a bill while accepting others (the so-called line-item veto), the president of the United States has no such choice. Thus the veto, though powerful, is clumsy.

President Carter would have to reject the entire $10.2 billion bill just to eliminate 18 projects worth less than 2 percent of the measure. In the process he also would very likely upset members concerned about parts of the bill that had nothing to do with the matter at issue, but that would still suffer the same veto.

Even as the bill was moving toward the House floor, a move to cut the 17 projects still in it was being planned by Rep. Silvio O. Conte of Massachusetts, ranking minority member of the House Appropriations Committee. Conte, whose district spans the hills, valleys, woods, and small towns of the Connecticut Valley, is known as an outdoorsman with a respect for the natural environment. He has clashed frequently with colleagues and administrations over what he considers wasteful and environmentally harmful water projects. As one of 72 representatives and senators who had signed a letter to President Carter on February 14 expressing support for his efforts to "reform the water resources program," Conte was prepared to back the president as far as he could. He teamed up with Rep. Butler C. Derrick, Jr. of South Carolina to offer an amend-

5

ment on the House floor to knock out 17 "boondoggle" water projects. The odds were heavily against their success.

The House Appropriations Committee is divided into 13 subcommittees, each of which exercises jurisdiction over specific agencies and functions of the federal government. These subcommittees hold almost exclusive and unchallenged sway over their domains, with most of the spending decisions being worked out among the members within each subcommittee. Because it is almost unheard of for one subcommittee to challenge the spending bill prepared by another, the full House Appropriations Committee rarely meets as a body except to complete the necessary motions of ratifying and sending to the full House the spending bill prepared by each of the subcommittees. In preparing its bill the Public Works Subcommittee had held 26 days of hearings in ten weeks, published ten volumes of testimony totaling 10,313 pages, and heard from 413 witnesses.

The 1978 public works and energy appropriations bill carried a price tag of $10.2 billion. It was said to be the largest public works spending proposal since Congress had first appropriated $75,000 in 1824 to clear snags and sandbars on the Ohio and Mississippi rivers. More than half the money in the bill, $5.9 billion, was for some aspect of energy research and development. There were funds for fossil, solar, geothermal, and fusion energy research. There were funds for nuclear research and applications programs—reactor technology development, space applications, assessments of environmental effects, as well as programs involving theoretical and experimental physics, materials and fuels technology, and instrumentation.

The bill also carried funds for military applications of nuclear energy, reactors for nuclear-powered naval vessels, uranium-enrichment activities, and weapons. Included in this portion of the bill were funds for the enhanced-radiation warhead, better known as the neutron bomb. A weapon described as able to kill people without destroying property, it had caused considerable controversy and some alarm because of its implications among those concerned about nuclear conflict in the world.

Even so, of the 413 witnesses who had appeared before the subcommittee that spring, 333 were there in connection with the water projects controversy. They included 107 members of the House, nearly one-fourth of the entire body. The real question was never whether the Conte-Derrick amendment could win (even they knew it would lose). The key question was, by how much? Would

6

enough members support the amendment to signal that a veto by President Carter would not be overridden in the House? The bill was scheduled for consideration on Monday and Tuesday, June 13 and 14, an indication of its importance as an issue since most legislation is disposed of in one day or less on the House floor.

Nearly 60 percent of the $10.2 billion public works spending bill for 1977 did not involve public works projects for water resources. Of the 505 such projects funded in the bill, the Conte-Derrick amendment sought to delete 17; a total of $176.4 million was involved, less than 2 percent of the entire bill, or 4 percent of that portion not devoted to energy research and development.

The House spent the better part of two legislative days on this measure, during which 84 members spoke about some aspect of the bill. Of these members, 75 (about 89 percent) spoke about the Conte-Derrick amendment or some aspect of it. Of 74 pages in the *Congressional Record* devoted to the overall appropriation bill, 54 pages (about 73 percent) were on the 17 projects covered by the amendment. In other words, 73 percent of the floor debate was devoted to 2 percent of the bill.

Much of that debate centered on three issues:

1. The prerogative of Congress to determine, through its traditional procedures, the spending priorities embodied in the bill.
2. The need to set and abide by more relevant, realistic, and objective criteria for approving public works projects.
3. The merits and demerits of the 17 projects at issue.

Following are excerpts from the congressional debate over four of the disputed projects:

Russell Dam and Lake Project

Of this $276 million project on the Savannah River between Georgia and South Carolina, Rep. Derrick, whose South Carolina district adjoined the project site, said in a rare burst of candor:

> I cannot ask taxpayers in California, New York, or Nebraska to pay for a project located in my district which is not worthy of further construction. . . . It is difficult to vote against a project in one's own home district. . . . But we have to start where it is hard first.

However, his senior colleague in the Senate, J. Strom Thurmond, simply said, "This dam will be built. It will be built sooner or later. Why not go ahead now, before costs go up?" (Thurmond later would prove to be both right and wrong; the dam would be built, but at double the 1977 cost figure.)

Oahe Irrigation Project

This $504.6 million project in South Dakota would divert water from the Missouri River through a 5,000-mile system of canals and channels to irrigate 190,000 acres for farming. In the process, 90,000 acres already under cultivation would be destroyed.

Local responsibility for implementing the project was with a local agency whose board of directors was publicly elected. The board had signed a contract with the U.S. Army Corps of Engineers under which terms for constructing the project, and repayments to the federal government, were established. In a 1976 election, however, the board of directors that had favored the projects and signed the contract was swept out of office and replaced by a new group, consisting of opponents of the project. They quickly announced that they would not continue to implement the terms of the contract with the Corps of Engineers.

Sen. Mark O. Hatfield of Oregon, who supported President Carter's effort to delete this project, said the wave of local opposition, as evidenced in the election of the new board, constituted an excellent reason to drop it. Congress, he said, "cannot impose a project on an area where the major contractor [the local board] says 'we don't want to perform'."

But South Dakota's Sen. George McGovern termed that "tunnel vision," and said "there is not any issue which is going to come before the Senate this year that I am more personally concerned with."

Cache River Basin Project

This $93.2 million project would channelize the Cache River in northeastern Arkansas to speed drainage for flood control. In the process it would clear 170,000 acres of forest and wetlands for agriculture, and ultimately affect 790,000 acres of bottomlands. Rep. Bill Alexander of Arkansas called it an environmentally balanced plan that enjoyed strong support by the "vast majority" of people in the area.

Rep. Conte called it the "most glaring example" of the "environment be damned" doctrine he said was "clearly enunciated" in the

8

bill. The project was so "popular," he noted, that the Arkansas state legislature had passed a resolution opposing it, and nine states bordering the Mississippi River had joined in a lawsuit to stop it because of the potential environmental damage.

Lukfata Lake and Dam Project

This $31.5 million flood-control project in the Oklahoma district of former House Speaker Carl Albert would send 70 percent of its benefits to a single catfish farm, Conte said. Oklahoma, he added "is saturated with these federally supported projects."

Rep. Wesley W. Watkins, who represented that district, agreed it contained a number of lakes, but said one more was needed to "fulfill the honor and word of this body." Besides, he added, with $50 million going to "Communist Rumania" in foreign economic aid, "it is an insult to the people of the 3rd District of Oklahoma" to demand that their project meet any economic cost-benefit standard.

Rep. Bevill tried to set an elevated tone by describing his public works bill as a "vigorous response to the energy crisis which affects all of us and to the water crisis which threatens most of us." In a small touch of irony, he noted that the panel, "in an effort to comply with the President's fine leadership in restraining Federal spending," had reported a bill below the budget request.

The bill was $137 million below the administration's estimate, which the committee had accomplished by a slight cut across the board. As Rep. Conte later noted, however, this simply penalized the "meritorious" projects while allowing the "boondoggles" to continue.

Rep. Hamilton Fish, Jr. of New York appeared to have captured the essence of the argument, calling the projects at issue "bottom of the barrel . . . of dubious value . . . offering great expense for a small return, or worse, a windfall for a few."

Behind the need to preserve individual projects was the determination to protect the system that permitted such projects in the first place. Veteran California congressman Harold T. "Bizz" Johnson, chairman of the Public Works and Transportation Committee, which had originally authorized the projects now in the spending bill, declared:

> We in Congress have the right to decide what projects should be authorized and funded. To agree to this amendment today would

be a clear signal that Congress is willing to give up its right and turn it over to the Administration.

Rep. William H. Harsha of Ohio warned that a dangerous precedent would be set if the disputed projects were cut from the bill. It would leave Congress with "no viable role in water resources development. If this move is successful, there will be no need for those who find their projects on the next hit list to come to us for help."

At stake, said Rep. James Abdnor of South Dakota, was "the integrity of Congressional decision-making and Congressional prerogatives." Each project, he added, "has been thoroughly studied . . . [and] the decision to fund these projects resulted only from systematic and extensive deliberation."

Rep. Patricia Schroeder of Colorado, however, in whose state were 3 of the 17 disputed projects, was among a handful who took a very different view:

> Nothing in the Federal budget ought to be sacrosanct. The budget is . . . filled with many costly and perhaps worthwhile expenditures. But we cannot ask the taxpayer to buy everything for everyone. There just simply are not enough tax dollars to go around.

Rep. Abner J. Mikva of Illinois said it was time to end a policy that says "what is good for me and my district is good for you. You take care of me and I will take care of you and the country will have to worry about itself." He urged his colleagues to support a "coordinated national public works policy rather than the bifurcated, individual parochial policy of the past."

When the votes were tallied, Conte-Derrick had lost, as expected, but the 194–218 outcome indicated that the House would not be able to override a presidential veto.

Even before the bill got to the Senate, the Public Works Subcommittee chairman, Sen. John C. Stennis of Mississippi, was working to achieve a compromise with which both sides could live. Unknown publicly at the time, an understanding with the White House had been reached that if Stennis's subcommittee would delete 9 of the 17 offending projects, Carter would accept the bill. The Senate proposed cuts totaling $59.8 million of the $176.4 spending represented by the 17 projects for 1978.

Sen. Floyd K. Haskell of Colorado, angry that three of the projects cut were from his state while none were cut from states of senators on the Public Works Subcommittee, tried unsuccessfully to get all of the cuts restored on the Senate floor. Equally unsuccessful was the effort of Sen. Thomas J. McIntyre of New Hampshire to get the Senate to delete the other eight projects on the list.

In sum the president ended a battle that consumed the better part of his first year in office by accepting 34 percent of the cuts he had initially proposed. All told the cuts came to 0.6 percent of the public works appropriation for FY 1978.

While the battle may have been over, the war was not. The following spring Rep. Bevill's subcommittee restored funds in the FY 1979 money bill for eight of the nine deleted projects. Only the Grove Lake, Kans., project, the one project the House had initially dropped in 1977, stayed out. The $21 million for the eight projects represented only about 0.2 percent of the $10.3 billion measure, but it led to another major confrontation with President Carter.

At a news conference on June 13, 1978, the president said he would veto the bill unless the eight projects were eliminated. Two days later the House defied the threat, rejecting an effort by Rep. Robert W. Edgar of Pennsylvania to delete the projects from the bill. The 142–234 margin led some to believe that a veto could be overridden as 43 members who had supported the 1977 effort switched their votes. As President Carter promised, he vetoed the bill, but the House was unable to override it. Later, even as Congress was sending back a revised bill shorn of the offending projects, Rep. Bevill said of the administration's position, "We will give them every consideration next year," but "we will preserve the prerogatives of the Congress."

Furthermore, the Senate's Environment and Public Works Committee chairman, Sen. J. Bennett Johnston, Jr. of Louisiana warned that the Senate was "not agreeing to never again consider projects" on the president's list.

As this report was being prepared, five years after the fight, a quick survey of the 18 projects on President Carter's 1977 list revealed the following. First, of the nine projects that Congress refused to delete in 1977, three have been completed, two were nearing completion, and four were in the stage of being redesigned. For the five projects completed or under way, the total cost had risen from the 1977 estimate of $448 million to $738 million in 1983, an increase of about 65 percent. Second, of the nine projects that were deleted in 1977, that Rep. Bevill tried to restore, and that led to the veto in 1978, all but one had been stopped. The single survivor was the

Yatesville Lake project in Kentucky, where Rep. Carl D. Perkins, for 28 years chairman of the House Education and Labor Committee, had managed to keep this home-state project alive. The price tag for this project was up from $54 million to $97 million, an increase of 80 percent.

To protect the Yatesville Lake project from any future budgetary vagaries, Perkins inserted into the 1983 supplemental appropriations bill language that is now part of United States law, saying:

> Hereafter, notwithstanding any other provisions of law or of this Act, appropriations for the Yatesville Lake construction project made available by Public Law 97-257, Chapter V and Public Law 97-377, Title I, Section 140 (96 State. 1916) shall be obligated to construct the Yatesville Lake Project.

Translation: This facility will be built, no matter what.

The Ford administration's 1978 budget, as had budgets of previous administrations, itemized water development projects for which funding was requested. Each project was listed, along with the estimated total federal cost, prior amounts allocated, and the amount needed to complete construction.

Someone apparently decided, however, that that was too much candor. Beginning with the next year, that section of the federal budget submitted to Congress has contained only a series of summary paragraphs by type of project, listing the total amount requested and the number of projects affected.

Military Bases: "Preserved, Protected, and Defended"

Out on rocky, scrub-brush terrain near Salt Lake City squats historic old Fort Douglas, built back in 1862 to straddle the overland stage route. More than half a continent away, in Virginia, on a peninsula between Hampton Roads and Chesapeake Bay, sprawls Fort Monroe, one of the few remnants of the War of 1812 and the only active-duty army post left in the nation, and maybe even in the world, that is protected by an 8-foot-deep moat.

What Fort Douglas and Fort Monroe have in common, besides their status as historical anomalies occupied by active-duty military contingents, is having withstood repeated attempts by the Department of Defense (DOD) since the mid-1960s to have each closed and transformed into a museum. Their survival as military bases underscores the potence and persistence of the congressional parochial imperative.

Few would argue that all of DOD's more than 5,000 installations and properties worldwide are necessary, efficient, or economical. In fact the argument, no matter who makes it, generally goes the opposite way; namely that some proportion of those facilities and of the estimated $20 billion a year spent to operate them are resources that could be better utilized elsewhere.

No better demonstration of why costly and unneeded military bases remain open has emerged recently than that provided by the senior senator from Texas, John G. Tower. He invited each of his 99 colleagues to provide a list by March 1, 1983, of military installations and programs in his or her state that could be trimmed because they are "not essential for national defense." As chairman of the Senate Armed Services Committee, Tower suspected that pork had wormed its way into the defense budget, and that the only way to excise it was for each member to rise above parochial concerns and take the national interest to heart.

By the deadline, only six senators had responded. Their combined proposals for savings in their own states totaled less than $200 million, of which not one penny involved a military facility from their own state or that of any other member. Their proposals were as follows:

- Sen. David Pryor of Arkansas suggested deleting funding for chemical weapons production in his state.
- Sen. Robert J. Dole of Kansas proposed the expedited removal of all Titan missiles at McConnell Air Force Base in his state.
- Sen. Charles McC. Mathias, Jr. of Maryland counseled the cancellation of the B-1 bomber program.
- Sen. Carl Levin of Michigan called for elimination of the B-1 bomber program, as well as the extremely low frequency communications defense program.
- Sen. Thomas F. Eagleton of Missouri proposed an across-the-board reduction in defense spending.
- Although Sen. J. James Exon of Nebraska suggested no specific reductions, he assured Tower that "we Nebraskans are belt-tighteners by nature."

Every state, and almost 60 percent of all congressional districts, contain or are adjacent to military bases or other installations. The payrolls and procurements associated with these military bases, an American Enterprise Institute analysis concluded, "may provide greater benefits [to communities and members of Congress] than do highly sought after projects for the construction of dams or the improvement of rivers and harbors."

The Office of Secretary of Defense PPSSCC Task Force, which studied the Defense Department, came up with what it described as a conservative estimate that $2 billion could be saved annually if a national base realignment and closure program were undertaken. Periodically, since 1981, the Congressional Budget Office has issued studies and reports suggesting that Congress pursue just such a program to help reduce the budget deficit. The General Accounting Office has made similar pleas in connection with its own base studies. All to no avail. The intoxicating allure of the parochial imperative has been simply too seductive, and the will of Congress to resist too weak, for the national interest to triumph.

Not since 1979, when its last national plan was micromanaged to death in Congress (much like the Carter administration's water projects hit list was handled) has the Defense Department offered any proposed overhaul of the military base status quo. Of 17 military installations formally slated by DOD for closure since 1977, a *Wall Street Journal* article in July 1982 reported that Congress had succeeded at keeping all but three from being shut down.

Until 20 years ago, it was a different era. DOD experienced relatively little congressional resistance when it sought to make a case that the retention of inefficient, costly, and misplaced facilities was not in the national interest. What provoked the change in attitudes? What factors prompted Congress to institutionally challenge, and subsequently handcuff, the executive branch's powers over the nation's military structure? Some clues may be found by examining the chronology of events leading up to the paralysis of the present day.

Back When DOD Had an Almost Free Hand

On December 12, 1963, Secretary of Defense Robert S. McNamara announced the closings of 33 military installations, a move intended to save an estimated $106 million a year. It was the first time in anyone's memory that a nationwide base realignment plan had been advanced publicly with so many proposed closings.

Reaction was immediate and widespread. As the *Washington Post* reported on the day after the announcement, "Wounded Congressmen rushed to the floor, some with a chart of their economically hit district in one hand and a warning of political retribution in the other." In Chicago, where the Fifth Army Headquarters was to be removed, Mayor Richard J. Daley convened the city's congressional delegation with orders to halt the relocation no matter what strings had to be pulled.

Rep. F. Edward Hebert of Louisiana, whose district was slated to lose an army camp and a supply depot, took the news more philosophically: "I've been preaching economy for all these years and I'm not going to start screaming now just because they shut down something in my backyard."

"The defense establishment should not be frozen into a permanent WPA," said Sen. George McGovern of South Dakota on introducing a bill to develop economic reconversion of communities affected by base closings. "We must be prepared to accept defense cuts resulting from shifts in emphasis [and not engage in] angry resistance to every proposal to protect the American taxpayers."

Little more than two weeks after the 1964 presidential election, Secretary McNamara announced the closure or reduction of 95 more bases and installations. When added to previous closings, these represented $1 billion in estimated annual savings. Before McNamara left the Pentagon for home on the day of the announcement, 169 members of Congress, by McNamara's count, had phoned him wanting explanations. As the *New York Daily News* editorialized, "The fact is that most of the installations which have come under the McNamara ax would have been phased out 10 years ago but for political pressures."

Alabama congressman Jack Edwards, however, said the new round of closings were "part of a plan to disarm this nation unilaterally." And, while Sen. Richard B. Russell of Georgia said he would "gladly support any action" by McNamara that "would reduce the staggering cost of the Department of Defense," Russell said the closing of Hunter Air Force Base in his state "is totally unjustified and I shall challenge this decision vigorously."

On May 26, 1965, the House Armed Services Committee added an amendment to a military construction bill authored by committee chairman L. Mendel Rivers of South Carolina that would endow the committee with final approval over DOD base closings. Passed along with it was an amendment by Massachusetts congressmen Edward P. Boland and Silvio O. Conte denying funds for construction of an arms development plant at the Rock Island (Ill.) arsenal, because the plant would be undertaking programs carried out by the Springfield (Mass.) armory, which DOD had ordered closed.

Two weeks later, the entire House went along with Rep. Rivers and voted to give itself legislative veto power over all pending and future base closings or reductions. The Senate passed a similar provision by voice vote at the urging of Sen. J. Strom Thurmond of South Carolina. In effect Congress had challenged the executive branch to a showdown over which would have ultimate authority to structure the nation's military.

On August 21, 1965, President Lyndon Johnson vetoed the military construction bill because of this base closing language, which he described as "a clear violation of the separation of powers."

Three months later, perhaps to underscore the president's point, Secretary McNamara announced the reduction or closing of 149 more military bases, for additional savings of $410 million a year. Thirty-nine states were affected by this new round of closings. McNamara insisted that Congress "has no power to block the actions" and that, as in the past, he "would not be persuaded to change [these] decisions by any Congressional objections."

Congress had not given up. When the next military construction bill, that for FY 1967, emerged from a conference committee, a compromise had been hammered out specifying that "no base involving 250 or more persons can be closed without the decision first lying before the House and Senate Armed Services Committees for 30 days review." In September 1966 President Johnson signed this legislation into law, but nonetheless he voiced "serious doubts" about the wisdom of giving Congress a 30-day review period over base closure decisions. But the escalation of the Vietnam War required closer cooperation with Congress, and this seemed at the time a small price to pay for congressional acquiescence in other areas. Thus the first precedent for Congress' intervention in military management on a massive scale found its way into law.

The Nixon administration on October 27, 1969, proposed the largest single base realignment package in history, a $3 billion economy move that involved the reduction or closing of 307 military installations. At first, reaction seemed muted compared to the furor such decisions had created during the Johnson years. The two senators from New York, Jacob K. Javits and Charles E. Goodell, did issue a joint statement vowing to fight any closures in their state. Generally, though, the rhetoric was more subdued, even statesmanlike. Sen. Philip A. Hart of Michigan set the high public tone: "I can do nothing but applaud these cuts even though they cause pain in my constituency. We would all be very poorly served by a military establishment which continued to operate bases it didn't need."

While public reaction seemed mild, behind-the-scenes lobbying and cajoling apparently soon jerked the Nixon administration back from its ambitious base realignment plans. On January 21, 1971, Secretary of Defense Melvin R. Laird let it be known that the White House had scrapped its plan for nationwide realignment. The "stay of execution" was ascribed to "a sagging national economy and rising unemployment." It marked the first time that an entire base realignment package had been withdrawn.

A second but far more limited attempt at realignment was made in April 1973, when Secretary of Defense Elliot L. Richardson announced 274 separate actions designed to save $500 million annually. In response, Sen. Claiborne Pell of Rhode Island and Sen. Edward M. Kennedy of Massachusetts, along with Massachusetts congressmen Thomas P. O'Neill, Jr. and Silvio O. Conte, introduced legislation to establish a commission to review the proposed closing of any military installation and to force the Secretary of Defense to submit to Congress justifications for each reduction or closing 180 days prior to that action. This legislation failed to pass.

One of the proposed consolidations to be studied from that 1973 realignment package involved closing one of the U.S. Army's two East Coast basic training centers, Fort Dix in New Jersey or Fort Jackson in South Carolina. Even as the study for closure progressed up through early 1975, congressional pressure to thwart a closure decision affecting either base intensified.

A headline in one South Carolina newspaper screeched: PROPOSED STUDY LOOKS TOWARD POSSIBLE FT. JACKSON CLOSING. HOLLINGS SAYS PREPOSTEROUS. Sen. Ernest F. Hollings along with Sen. Thurmond organized their state's lobbying counterattack. Thurmond repeatedly pointed out that the army had spent $165 million on Fort Jackson for construction since 1964, compared to just $84 million spent on Fort Dix. Cost alone, he argued, made Fort Dix a more reasonable candidate for closure.

New Jersey's congressional delegation, led by Sen. Harrison A. Williams, Jr. and Rep. Frank Thompson, Jr., lured Secretary of the Army Howard H. Callaway to Fort Dix for an inspection that was designed to spotlight the base's newly constructed reception and detention centers.

Even though the army study eventually concluded that Fort Dix should be closed, thanks to its spirited congressional support it remained open and survived yet another attempt at closure in 1979.

Meanwhile, using a series of legislative vehicles, the House and Senate armed services committees had launched a coordinated attack to further limit executive branch authority over base realignments. Tacked onto the FY 1977 military construction authorization was Section 612. This section prohibited any base closure or reduction of more than 250 civilian employees until DOD had notified Congress of "candidate" actions, assessed the personnel and economic impacts, followed the study provisions of the National Environmental Policy Act, and waited nine months.

The House and Senate conference report for FY 1977 military construction made Section 612 retroactive to include closure studies from a year earlier, such as Fort Devens in Massachusetts, Fort Indiantown Gap and the New Cumberland Army Depot in Pennsylvania, Loring Air Force Base in Maine, and Webb Air Force Base in Texas. The report said: "The conferees are confident that this provision will improve base realignment procedures. It does not represent a violation of the principle of the separation of powers."

When the legislation reached President Ford's desk for signature, he vetoed it, contending that a president "must be able, if the need arises, to change or reduce the mission at any military installation if and when that becomes necessary."

The House voted to override President Ford's veto by 270 to 131. On the Senate side, Sen. John G. Tower of Texas, in whose state were several bases targeted for extinction, pleaded that "it is essential Congress have the right to review base closings." Nevertheless the override effort fell 11 votes short in the Senate.

Beginning in February 1977, with a new president in office, several bills were introduced in a concerted effort to widen the scope of congressional control. Rep. William S. Cohen of Maine, along with Rep. Norman Y. Mineta of California and Rep. Robert E. Bauman of Maryland, introduced a bill to require DOD to report closures or reductions to Congress, and to prepare, in addition to National Environmental Policy Act reports, a study on the local economic and environmental consequences of every proposed action. The bill included language making it retroactive to the previous year, when DOD had announced its latest closings. Rep. Jim Leach of Iowa and Rep. Tom Railsback of Illinois introduced a bill to require closure reports in advance and five consecutive years of analysis of cost savings following any closures or reductions.

Sen. Donald W. Riegle, Jr. of Michigan and 31 cosponsors in the House, including Reps. John D. Dingell and David A. Stockman of Michigan, introduced bills to require DOD to provide communities affected by closures or reductions with 10 percent of total projected savings from the realignment action for a period of 10 years. (This would have been in addition to other federal assistance available to impacted communities under the interdepartmental Economic Adjustment Committee established in 1970).

In August 1977 Congress enacted legislation requiring DOD to notify Congress when a base is a candidate for reduction or closure, and that DOD also prepare local economic, environmental, and strategic consequence reports and wait 60 days for Congress' response. President Carter then signed this restriction of his powers into law.

On April 26, 1978, Secretary of Defense Harold Brown released a list of 85 base reductions, realignments, and closings he estimated would save $337 million annually. Congressional opposition was widespread, vociferous, and united. One by one, entire congressional delegations issued statements vowing resistance.

Rep. Philip M. Crane of Illinois, for instance, described the decision to close Fort Sheridan, in Chicago's northern suburbs, as "callous and insensitive." From the adjoining district, Rep. Robert McClory vowed to "vigorously oppose any attempt to close Fort Sheridan. Many of the employees who work there live in my district." Sen. Charles H. Percy said he was "shocked" by the proposed closing and pledged to battle President Carter "every step of the way." Only Sen. Adlai E. Stevenson parted company with his state's congressional delegation, saying Fort Sheridan "should be studied for possible use as a park and for housing for the elderly."

With the military construction authorization of FY 1980, the House Armed Services Committee inserted a warning to DOD: "The Committee wishes to emphasize that because of the effects of base closings, the Department of Defense is put on notice that it must comply fully with the provisions of the National Environmental Policy Act of 1969 and 10 U.S.C. 2687, be prepared to justify any final closure and realignment actions, and be prepared for committee review and scrutiny of such actions."

The House and Senate conference report on military construction went even further. It singled out five bases that had been on the DOD list—Fort Dix in New Jersey, Goodfellow Air Force Base in Texas, Fort Indiantown Gap and the New Cumberland Army Depot in Pennsylvania, and Fort Monroe in Virginia—and directed that in each case no closure or realignment could take place unless impact statements were prepared that "place special emphasis on socio-economic factors in the affected area." Even in instances where environmental impact statements had already been prepared supporting the decision to close, such as in the case of Fort Monroe, the conference report directed that DOD should "carefully review" the statements with regard to socio-economic impacts and "if necessary" they "should be revised or amended."

What this language translates into is the directive: "Thou Shalt Not Close." Sitting on that conference committee were members with vested interests in the five facilities singled out, including Sen. John G. Tower of Texas and Sen. John W. Warner and Rep. G. William Whitehurst of Virginia.

Soon after this frontal assault on executive prerogatives, other members of Congress started scrambling to insert restrictive language of their own into legislation. One instance occurred when, after a plea from Sen. Edmund S. Muskie of Maine, the Senate Armed Services Committee inserted into the FY 1980 military construction authorization bill language "prohibiting the realignment of Loring Air Force Base" in Maine. The committee emphasized that its decision to include this provision "derives from strategic considerations and not from the economic and social consequences . . . although such consequences are recognized and would require mitigation if the reduction were pursued." In another instance Rep. Thomas Loeffler of Texas, a member of the Appropriations Subcommittee on Military Construction, wrote into the FY 1982 military construction appropriation bill language giving Goodfellow Air Force Base, which happened to be in his district, $500,000 to design facilities that DOD had not requested. The base had been marked for closure, but the money Loeffler provided was to design two new training facilities and personnel housing.

In another example of the use of restrictive language, the entire Pennsylvania congressional delegation can claim credit for a provision in the 1982 House defense appropriations bill that directed that "the Army shall continue the maintenance of CH-47 helicopters at the New Cumberland Army Depot." In addition Sen. Daniel K. Inouye of Hawaii made certain the FY 1983 supplemental appropriations bill contained a section "which prohibits the use of funds for the sale, lease, rental, or excessing of any portion of land of Fort DeRussy, Honolulu, Hawaii." The 73-acre facility is an army reserve headquarters whose ranks had included only 143 personnel as of 1981.

News reports in May 1981 indicated that the Pentagon and the Reagan administration's Office of Management and Budget were compiling a list of 50 bases for closure. Within weeks of these news reports, congressional members of the Northeast-Midwest Coalition, representing over 200 members of Congress, were lobbying DOD and the White House for a moratorium on base closings in their region.

On February 26, 1982, the Reagan administration, under pressure from Congress, reversed itself and canceled a plan to close 15 coast guard stations in 11 states, which would have saved $31 million annually.

One year later, on February 15, 1983, the Associated Press reported:

> A key defense official says the Pentagon may haul out a list of proposed base closings and challenge congressmen to bear some of the brunt, "if the heat gets heavy" for deep cuts in the military budget.
>
> More than 18 months ago Defense Secretary Caspar Weinberger said the Pentagon planned to ask Congress for authority to close or realign some bases, but there was never a follow up. The list includes some bases the Pentagon has been trying to close for nearly a decade.
>
> There was a time, about 20 years ago, when the Pentagon had a virtually free hand in determining what bases to eliminate.

During testimony before the Senate Armed Services Committee on July 29, 1983, Secretary Weinberger challenged Congress to repeal restrictions it had imposed that "make it virtually impossible to close any military installation in this country, regardless of the merits of the case." Furthermore, said Weinberger, Congress should stop micromanaging administrative functions of the Pentagon, such as "telling me how to organize my staff."

Sen. Tower responded by saying Weinberger had "properly identified Congress as part of the problem." He went on, however, to claim a congressional prerogative to intervene because the Pentagon was "a vast, multilayered bureaucracy that is not as responsive as we would like it to be."

Congressional Ploys to Save Facilities

Imagination knows no bounds when a member of Congress feels compelled to become the self-appointed guardian or savior of a particular military facility. When legislative language blocking base closures or reductions seems inadequate, members have been known to resort to a veritable repertoire of maneuvers.

When DOD wanted to partially reduce the Lexington (Ky.) Bluegrass Army Depot in 1976 to save $37 million annually, Rep. John B. Breckinridge filed suit in federal court claiming that people must be included with trees and birds in any environmental impact statement prior to closure. The judge issued an injunction restraining DOD from closing the depot, but an appeals court later reversed the ruling.

When DOD wanted to move the Naval Resale Systems office from Brooklyn, N.Y. to Illinois in 1976, Rep. Elizabeth Holtzman and other members of the New York delegation convinced the General Services Administration (GSA) to reduce by one-third the rent it charged the navy office. "This in my judgement means that the Navy probably has no economic justification now for moving out of New York City," Holtzman declared. It did not seem to matter to her that the savings were illusory; robbing from Peter (the GSA) to pay Paul (the navy) only shifted the cost burden around.

When DOD wanted to close the Philadelphia Naval Shipyard in 1973, a goal that has eluded it repeatedly since at least 1959, Sen. Hugh Scott of Pennsylvania had to summon all of his cajoling powers. According to his version of events, that required only a visit to his old friend and fellow native Virginian, Secretary of the Navy John W. Warner. "I was among those who strongly recommended Warner for Undersecretary of the Navy," Senator Scott explained to the *Philadelphia Bulletin* that year. "When the secretaryship came along, the Secretary of Defense [Melvin Laird] assured me I was backing the right horse [Warner]."

Phone calls, visits, political trade-offs, and other lobbying pressures often combine to keep bases open without resort to the legislative process. Not even DOD knows for certain how many bases Congress has saved from closure. A memorandum sent to the secretary of defense by the assistant secretary for manpower, reserve affairs and logistics, and obtained by the Office of Secretary of Defense PPSSCC Task Force, reads in part: "There probably have been other cases where Congressional pressure has been put on the military departments that influenced their decision to maintain the status quo, but since these actions never come to DOD's attention, we do not know the total number of bases that Congress precluded us from closing."

The list of bases Congress has rescued is lengthy, but at least half a dozen stand out from the rest as survivors of a particularly rare and hardy breed.

Fort Douglas. First scheduled for closing on November 20, 1964, Fort Douglas had its obituary read three more times—in 1970, 1978, and 1979—before DOD finally relented in 1981 and announced that the 121-year-old fort would retain active military status. Over the years the fort's area had been reduced from 7,898 acres to the present 119 acres.

The army estimated it would achieve savings of $792,000 annually from closure, with one-time closure costs of $2.56 million. This estimate was challenged by Sen. E. J. ("Jake") Garn of Utah, who had become Fort Douglas's principal proponent and protector during his years in the Senate. Garn requested a General Accounting Office (GAO) audit of the army's base realignment plan in 1979, claiming the army's savings projections had understated closure costs. The GAO came back with an estimated annual savings from closure of $580,000, and one-time closure costs of $2.65 million— only $90,000 more than what the army had estimated for closure. From his position on the Defense Appropriations Subcommittee, Garn added a section in the FY 1981 bill for military construction denying DOD the $2.2 million it had requested as a revised estimate for the closure costs of Fort Douglas. "The Committee recognizes that the denial of these funds will likely delay the proposed realignment action," read the section, which went on to direct the army to prepare an "alternative use study" for the fort.

In early 1981, when rumors indicated that Fort Douglas was on a list of proposed base closures prepared by the newly installed Reagan administration, Sen. Garn swung back into action on the issue. He wrote a letter to President Reagan on March 3, 1981, signed by ten other members of Congress, including Sen. Orrin G. Hatch of Utah and Rep. Dan Marriott of Utah urging that Fort Douglas be retained as an active army post. They argued that their own investigation, conducted by the House Committee on Appropriations, differed with findings of the army and GAO investigators on the most important point—annual savings. The lawmakers claimed the closure of Fort Douglas would not save a penny, and instead would actually *cost* $344,979 annually. At this point DOD apparently exhausted its patience for closure. In the FY 1984 budget Garn obtained $910,000 to construct a new entryway processing station, giving Fort Douglas still another lease on life.

Fort Monroe. The nation's only base with a moat around it was significantly reduced in 1970, studied for closure in 1978, and announced for execution in 1979. Three reasons were most often cited for closure: The fort is too old, too small, and constitutes a single-mission post, which means it is no longer what DOD calls "cost effective." It is a fort better suited as a museum for tourists than as a museum occupied by military personnel. The Pentagon estimated $10 million a year in savings if the fort's occupants, made up of the 2,900-member staff of the army's training and doctrine command, were transferred to another post only a short distance away.

When the 1979 closure order came down, Rep. Paul S. Trible, Jr. of Virginia, whose district encompassed the post, launched a lobbying campaign from his seat on a House subcommittee overseeing military facilities. An environmental impact study was ordered, and congressional auditors were dispatched to question statistics DOD used in its closure decision. Language appeared in the military construction appropriations bill demanding a "socio-economic impact statement" on the effect of Fort Monroe's closing.

Delay after delay ensued, thereby preventing closure, until finally a regulatory provision helped save the post. Fort Monroe had been declared a national historic monument in 1961, but before it could ever be opened to the public, dud ammunition that had been buried on the premises would have to be removed. The projected cost of removal ranged from the army's 1979 estimate of $2.5 million to a figure Rep. Trible endorsed of $32.3 million. This would have included searching not only the moat for munitions and historic artifacts, but digging up the entire post, under asphalt and concrete. Even though Pentagon auditors were highly dubious of the cleanup cost figure—after all, only $9 million had been spent to remove explosives from the grounds of the closed Frankford Arsenal in Philadelphia—DOD finally relented, if only to avoid future headaches.

DOD's decision amounted to tacit acceptance of a form of twisted logic, namely that essentially Fort Monroe can never be closed because it will always be more expensive to shut down than keep open, in terms of the short-term savings to be gained. That the army's estimated $10 million annual savings from closure would pay back the cleanup costs in less than four years seems not to have swayed the decision. In both the FY 1979 and FY 1981 military appropriations bills, $550,000 in new construction money was provided for Fort Monroe.

Loring Air Force Base. Loring Air Force Base in Maine experienced reductions in 1970, 1974, and 1979. The 1979 amendment to the Senate military construction bill, advanced by Sen. Edmund S. Muskie, of Maine, prohibited any further reduction of the base. It was later dropped, though, in a Senate-House conference after Secretary of Defense Harold Brown promised to keep Loring fully operational. Muskie and Maine's other senator, William Cohen, urged the local "Keep Loring Committee," composed of civic leaders and Loring employees, to continue pressing the Air Force to make major improvements to the base. The strategy was simple: the more tax money pumped into the base for improvements, the less justification for future reductions or a closing. Cohen's seat on the Senate Armed Services Committee gave him a vantage point from which to bring about these improvements for Loring Air Force Base:

- FY 1981: $24.5 million appropriated for new and improved personnel housing.
- FY 1982: $12.3 million appropriated for plane maintenance.
- FY 1983: $52.1 million appropriated for family housing, waste treatment, energy conservation, and other facilities.
- FY 1984: $36.4 million appropriated for personnel housing, alert runway, maintenance complex, and alterations.

A total of $125.3 million in appropriations has accumulated at Loring Air Force Base since the Cohen-Muskie lobbying plea.

Goodfellow Air Force Base. Goodfellow Air Force Base in San Angelo, Tex., was slated for reductions in 1970 and 1973. Closure was studied in 1978 and announced on March 29, 1979. The air force death notice described Goodfellow as "a small single-mission base with a relatively high per capital operating cost." Closure would save an estimated $14 million annually. In January 1971, soon after the first announced major reduction had seemed to doom the base, the Texas senators, John G. Tower and Lloyd M. Bentsen, engaged in a frantic lobbying campaign to save it. Tower was soon quoted in the *Dallas Times Herald* as saying that "Our labors to save Goodfellow have borne fruit."

The more serious threat developed in 1978, when closure seemed imminent. Rep. Thomas Loeffler, whose district encompassed the base, introduced an amendment to the military construction bill to force DOD to prepare a full environmental impact statement, a process that could cost up to $1 million and delay closure for at least a year. DOD insisted such a statement was unnecessary in the Goodfellow case. Tower and Bentsen requested an extension on the public comment period. Loss of Goodfellow, said Tower, "would be a major national security risk." Bentsen called Goodfellow "vital to our nation's defense."

With Tower as chairman of the Armed Services Committee beginning in 1981, and Loeffler on the House Appropriations Committee, Goodfellow's future became more assured. In FY 1983, $15.3 million was appropriated for an intelligence training facility and enlisted personnel housing at Goodfellow. In FY 1984, $10 million was appropriated for real estate acquisition, a voice-processing training facility, and fire protection systems at the base. A total of $25.3 million has been absorbed by Goodfellow since Sen. Tower assumed the Armed Services Committee chairmanship.

Fort Sheridan. This 729-acre lakefront facility north of Chicago was scheduled for reductions in 1969 and 1974, with closure studied in both 1978 and 1979. The army expected to reap $30 million just from the sale of this prime real estate, which included a golf course and numerous historical buildings dating back to the fort's founding in 1877. Soon after announcement of the first proposed reduction, Rep. Robert McClory of Illinois undertook to limit the impact by staying in regular contact with Secretary of the Army Stanley R. Resor. McClory and five other congressmen introduced legislation to require congressional oversight of any DOD actions to relocate military facilities. In February 1971 McClory was able to state: "I have been assured that earlier plans to close the fort have been rescinded."

Ten years later, when behind-the-scenes moves to close Fort Sheridan were under way, Rep. McClory and Illinois' senators, Charles H. Percy and Alan J. Dixon, conferred with Defense Secretary Weinberger. "We pressed our case about Fort Sheridan," McClory told the *Chicago Tribune* in May 1981. "I am sure now it will not be closed." To make certain, McClory sent a letter to President Reagan on September 10, 1981, calling Fort Sheridan "one of the most beautiful and serviceable military posts in the nation," with an army museum, a brig, a cemetery, and a golf course. "Approximately 1,600 civilian employees," wrote McClory, "a large percentage of which are minority citizens, would find housing location an extreme hardship should the base be removed."

A little over a year later, in December 1982, the army relented and formally announced that Fort Sheridan would not be closed because of "the disruption and adverse effect the removal of the Army's presence in the Chicago area" would have. In essence a tacit admission had been made that Fort Sheridan, and by extension the entire military base structure, constituted an economic and jobs program.

Chanute Air Force Base. A closure study of Chanute Air Force Base, located in central Illinois, began in 1978. An air force statement at the time indicated a need to reduce the number of bases dedicated to technical training, with Chanute as a prime candidate for closure since it "is the sole single-mission technical training base and could possibly be closed with comparatively limited disruption of activities." Estimated savings would amount to $40 million a year.

"I will vigorously fight the Air Force every step of the way," vowed Rep. Edward R. Madigan who represented the area. Senators Percy and Stevenson also pledged their support. Rep. Madigan said he was seeking pointers on how to prevent the closing from "Rep. Don Mitchell of New York, who successfully overturned a decision to close Griffis AFB at Rome, New York." Sen. Percy met with President Carter and pleaded for the base on the grounds that the economic impact of closing "would be immense." The Champaign, Ill., school district stood to lose $55,000 a year and the nearby Urbana school district $26,000 a year in impact aid if the base were closed, in addition to the loss of civilian base jobs.

Meanwhile, a $7.4 million appropriation for a sewage plant at the base was being held up pending a resolution of the closure issue. Although there was no use spending the money on a facility about to be shut down, Rep. Madigan, apparently acting on good advice from Rep. Mitchell, sought to pry the funds loose, urging the Illinois Environmental Protection Agency to push for the money in order to "stop Chanute from polluting." Quick acquisition of the sewage plant money, reasoned a *Champaign-Urbana News Gazette* editorial, "would strengthen greatly the case against closing Chanute."

The air force strategy then shifted to pitting Chanute against Lowry Air Force Base in Colorado as a candidate for closure. With a sort of divide-and-conquer strategy of setting one congressional delegation against another, the prospects seemed brighter for accomplishing the closure of at least one of the two bases. Assistant Air Force Secretary Antonia Chayes assured the Colorado delegation that "Chanute is still the prime candidate for closure, but Lowry is second." Rep. William L. Armstrong expressed his concern to her that the air force would buckle "to political pressure from Senator Percy and Congressman Madigan." The assistant secretary responded that environmental and cost studies rather than politics would dictate which base would be closed.

In September 1978 the results of the air force study were made public: $14 million more would be saved by closing Chanute than by shutting down Lowry. Asked whether he would now go along with the closing of Chanute if it were shown to be in the national interest, Rep. Madigan replied: "The preponderance of evidence would indicate that a showing like that would be impossible to arrive at." On March 15, 1979, Pentagon officials informed Rep. Madigan that Chanute had been taken off the "endangered species" list of proposed closures. Since this announcement, federal dollars have descended on Chanute in the following deluge:

- FY 1981: $14.6 million for personnel housing and a heating plant.
- FY 1982: $8.7 million for repairs and improvements and an energy program.
- FY 1983: $23.1 million for a gymnasium, personnel housing, and alterations to the waste treatment plant.
- FY 1984: $89.2 million for a maintenance training facility, a central heating plant, and repairs.

The total comes to $135.6 million appropriated, further ensuring that Chanute Air Force Base has a long and expensive future.

The Impact Aid Justification

As in the case of Chanute Air Force Base, the loss of federal impact aid dollars—assistance provided to school districts containing federal facilities—provokes almost as much consternation as the loss of civilian jobs. Sometimes it produces quandaries and conflicts for members of Congress, who on the one hand vehemently oppose a base closing in their district, while on the other hand arguing that the base creates a federal student burden on the local school district that necessitates more impact aid.

Every administration since that of President Harry S Truman has proposed the reduction or elimination of impact aid, but Congress has never cooperated. Over the last five years alone, the cumulative additional cost of higher funding levels appropriated by Congress over and above the administration's requests amounts to $1.2 billion.

In the National Interest

It is perhaps instructive to note the following excerpt from an editorial in a March 22, 1976, edition of the *Philadelphia Inquirer*, which appeared after an announcement that Philadelphia would lose a naval hospital and a DOD clothing factory to closure:

> The U.S. Department of Defense has many missions, but combating unemployment isn't one of them. Nor is it the Pentagon's function to subsidize the local economy in any community by maintaining military facilities regardless of need.

Commissaries: "Government in the Grocery Store Business"

Consider the following excerpts from the October 14, 1983, issue of "Bolling Beam," the newspaper of Bolling Air Force Base in Washington, D.C.:

> "If you want to save money on your food bill, now's the time to do it," says John L. McDonald, Bolling's Commissary Officer. The Bolling Commissary is slashing prices on nearly 500 items during its celebration of the Air Force Commissary Service's Seventh Anniversary.
>
> "Our customers normally save 25 to 34 percent by shopping here instead of in civilian stores and with this [one month] sale they can expect to save an additional 15 to 25 percent." No limit has been placed on the amount of sale items that can be purchased. Those requesting large quantities in case lots should call a day ahead of time.
>
> Thanks to a recent $450,000 "enhancement" project, McDonald continues, "we've expanded the deli, added a bigger bakery, added a health food center and lots of other customer convenience features."
>
> "Not many people realize it, but we do a lot of customized ordering to suit our customers' desires, especially in our meat department."

Six other military commissaries resembling the one at Bolling are located within the Washington, D.C., metropolitan area. At least

231 more commissaries like them are spread across the continental United States, servicing an ever-expanding clientele that includes not only active-duty military personnel and their families but also military retirees and the disabled, U.S. Public Health Service officers, certain National Oceanic and Atmospheric Administration personnel and American Red Cross workers, lighthouse keepers, housekeepers of military personnel, selected military personnel of foreign nations—and the list goes on and on.

Unlike the self-sufficient post exchanges, which operate as military base department stores selling goods at wholesale prices, the commissary system relies on a taxpayer subsidy that in FY 1983 had reached $590 million in direct appropriated costs, with another $168 million or more of indirect costs, according to the PPSSCC Privatization Task Force Study. This subsidy and over $4 billion in annual sales makes the commissary system one of the ten largest grocery store chains in the nation, and maybe in the world.

It is also the largest and perhaps only grocery chain in the world to have no statutory, or indeed compelling, market justification for existing in its present form. That such a system does exist and is able to perpetuate itself in competition with the private sector is a testament to its protectors in Congress.

When the system first began to evolve in the early 19th century, army posts generally were found only in isolated parts of the frontier. It was then reasonable to expect that food and other items should be provided at cost to compensate for the harsh and inaccessible conditions. With the establishment of each new service branch of the military, culminating with the air force in 1947, there emerged separate but similar commissary systems, each resembling a grocery store chain.

While the basic operations remained the same during this period, the needs and conditions that had originally justified them dramatically changed. By 1948 the four branches of the military had spawned 210 commissaries in the continental United States. A subcommittee of the House Armed Services Committee examined the entire system in hearings a year later and found that "remoteness" was no longer the guiding criterion for establishing commissaries. Many were operating within clearly defined metropolitan areas. "It was never intended that the Government should go in the business of providing for its personnel where they have the privilege and opportunity to go to a private place to buy," commented the committee chairman at the close of the hearings.

In response the DOD formulated three criteria to implement a regulation stating that "commissary stores shall not be authorized in areas where adequate commercial facilities are conveniently available. . . ." These criteria were that the food prices at commercial stores must be unreasonable, the commercial stores must be an unreasonable distance from the base, and the commercial stores must have an inadequate selection of goods. The criteria became the justifications for commissaries already in existence, as well as all future ones.

Congress restated its concern in July 1953, when the Senate Appropriations Committee reported: "The Committee fails to find any justification for the continuation of commissaries at military installations which are surrounded by or which abut metropolitan areas." That same year Congress directed the armed services to conduct a triennial certification of each commissary to eliminate those in metropolitan areas. For all practical purposes this was the last act of oversight Congress ever exercised over the commissary system.

More than ten years passed before anyone studied the problem again. A 1964 report to the Joint Economic Committee prepared by the GAO, Congress' own investigative watchdog agency, reported that the "criteria used to justify commissaries were unrealistic and did not meet the intent of the Congress." The evidence was clear. Of 49 commissaries built over the previous decade and a half, most were in metropolitan areas and had been justified on the flimsy basis that the prices at nearby commercial stores were not reasonable. Given the fact that market prices at these stores were being tested against the taxpayer-subsidized discount of 25 percent and more at commissaries, of course the commercial prices would seem unreasonable to those enjoying the discount.

These findings apparently fell on unreceptive ears. For when, 11 years later, in a March 1975 GAO report to the House Appropriations Committee, 27 of the continental U.S. commissaries were selected at random and studied, all were discovered to be within a five-mile radius of at least four large commercial food stores with competitive prices. Six commissaries in the Washington, D.C., metropolitan area, for example, were found to have 88 major grocery outlets within a three-mile radius. The GAO concluded: "Commissaries are not necessary at military installations in large metropolitan areas. . . . DOD's continued operation of commissaries in metropolitan areas cannot be justified. . . . If the Congress wishes DOD to continue commissary operations as a fringe benefit or for other reasons, the basis should be clearly stated in public law."

Two months later a follow-up GAO report to Congress revealed that no commissary had been closed since 1953 for failing to meet the criteria, mainly because "criteria used to justify commissaries are so structured as to perpetuate the commissaries." The GAO urged Congress to "take a close look at the need for maintaining commissary stores in competition with commercial grocery stores and at added expense to the taxpayer."

The Ford administration used the release of these two GAO reports as an opportunity to advance its budget proposal for phasing out the taxpayer subsidy. Under the Ford initiative commissaries would have to be 50 percent self-supporting by October 1, 1975, and fully self-supporting a year later. It seemed a modest proposal. No commissaries would be closed. Commissary patrons would still be able to purchase food at reduced cost, savings estimated by one Defense Department official at up to 15 percent or more. No one was even suggesting at this stage that commissaries be contracted out to commercial concerns: only that they be operated like the post exchanges—with all overhead and personnel costs paid for by the patrons. The savings to the American taxpayers from these direct appropriated subsidies alone would have been $324 million a year beginning in 1976.

When the Ford administration proposal reached the House Armed Services Committee, the resident members promptly derailed the bandwagon. Fifteen bills and resolutions were introduced opposing "any" change in the commissary funding status quo. Seven of the bills were submitted by Rep. G. William Whitehurst of Virginia, and they were cosponsored by such members with fiscally conservative reputations as Marjorie S. Holt and Robert E. Bauman of Maryland, Trent Lott of Mississippi, and William Nichols of Alabama.

Only Rep. Les Aspin of Wisconsin, who once served as an aide to the secretary of defense, introduced a bill to support the Ford initiative. Aspin implored his colleagues to eliminate a spending program that had outlived its usefulness:

> The direct and indirect subsidies to the military commissaries . . . which are protected from competition . . . total $440 million. This is twice as much as we are spending to fight the heroin traffic or find the causes of cancer. Yet this staggering sum is spent with

questionable legal justification and does nothing to contribute to our national security.

Notwithstanding Aspin's plea, the House Armed Services Committee voted 27 to 5 for House Concurrent Resolution 198, expressing opposition to any change in commissary funding.

For its fiscal year 1977 budget request, DOD proposed a three-year phaseout of the appropriated fund support for the labor-related costs of commissaries. Sen. Henry L. Bellmon of Oklahoma and Sen. John C. Culver of Iowa introduced an amendment to accomplish this goal. The debate and vote was held August 2, 1976. Here is a sampling of the statements from the Senate floor:

- Sen. Ted Stevens of Alaska: "My reasons for supporting continued funding revolve around the human element. I am particularly concerned with the effect of this proposed phase-out on the Alaska military community."
- Sen. Hiram L. Fong of Hawaii: "Over two million officers and men and women in uniform, their families, plus one million retirees and their families, plus some 29 million veterans—that is 32 or more million people and their families in the United States—have protested about the phase-out of commissary funding."
- Sen. Strom Thurmond of South Carolina: "It will not abolish the commissaries or close them entirely, I agree to that, but it will increase the prices. . . . This is a small fringe benefit."
- Sen. John C. Culver of Iowa: "The first-year savings alone provided by this amendment would more than cover the full annual operating costs of our strategic ICBM force plus our short-range attack missiles."

On a roll call vote the Bellmon-Culver amendment passed by one vote, 45–44. The split did not respect either party or ideological lines. Voting to retain the status quo were such penny pinchers as Sen. William Proxmire of Wisconsin and Sen. John G. Tower of Texas.

The House once again disapproved any change in the commissary system. And even in the Senate, after the elections of 1976, attitudes hardened again in favor of the status quo. In 1978 another attempt in the Senate to reduce the taxpayer burden to commissaries failed, this time by a vote of 59 to 33. A year later Sen. Bellmon and Sen. Jacob K. Javits of New York introduced legislation to give states and local governments the authority to collect excise taxes on alcohol and tobacco products sold in commissaries and exchanges. The Senate leadership, however, never allowed the measure to come up for a vote.

In January 1980 the GAO, acting once again as the conscience of Congress, issued still another report on commissaries. This was the GAO's fourth report, and the picture painted this time of Congress' oversight failures was even bleaker:

> Because of the large appropriated subsidy, the services have little incentive to operate commissaries economically. In 1977 DoD was operating with appropriated funds at least 109 . . . U.S. commissaries in metropolitan areas where food was conveniently available at reasonably competitive prices. . . . [Congress should] reduce the direct appropriated fund subsidy of commissary operations by prohibiting the use of appropriated funds to support commissaries in metropolitan areas . . . and Congress should enact legislation to provide a clear, legal basis for any future commissary operations.

Service officials claim they have a moral commitment to maintain commissaries as a routine fringe benefit for both active-duty and retired personnel. But, said the GAO, "this assumed moral commitment cannot be considered an obligation to maintain a commissary program of unchanging scope without regard to its cost or its need."

During 1981 a proposal emerged in the House Appropriations Committee to reduce the commissary subsidy by $15 million (a cut of less than 3 percent) and to increase the price of at-cost commissary liquor by 10 percent. Even this very modest change was squashed. As Rep. W. C. (Dan) Daniel of Virginia boasted, writing in the *Journal of the American Logistics Association* (Spring 1982): "We were fortunate in getting all of these funds restored. However, a very dangerous trend has been established. . . . Congress is attempting to establish artificially high prices for certain resale goods and use such funds to reduce the level of taxpayer support." Furthermore, Daniel warned his readers, the military services are "adding fuel to the fire" of attempts to reduce commissary funding by "its efforts to contract out commissaries. . . ."

When PPSSCC began releasing its preliminary findings early in 1983, the task force report dealing with the privatization of government services recommended the elimination of taxpayer subsidies to commissaries and advocated the contracting out of commissary services to the private sector to achieve even more cost savings. The reaction among those vested interests protecting the commissary status quo was swift and frenzied. Editorialized the *Exchange and Commissary News* in its August 15 1983, issue: "It's time for this market to wake up and stop waiting for the House Armed Services Committee to constantly stop everything negative from becoming law. Our associations and key industry leaders must anticipate rather than react to head off moves to contract out or close the commissaries."

It should be noted that one strategy for reinforcing the commissary status quo is to significantly expand the number of potential beneficiaries eligible to shop at commissaries. The more beneficiaries, the more pressure and votes that can be brought to bear against those reformers seeking to save tax dollars. Following soon after the announcement of PPSSCC findings on commissaries, three pieces of legislation were introduced that would go a long way toward this goal.

The first, submitted on June 13, 1983, by Sen. Paul S. Sarbanes of Maryland, would amend the U.S. Code to allow the use of commissary stores by all those persons who have left the military and are entitled to retired pay, but have not yet reached retirement age. The second bill, offered on July 13 by Senator Paul S. Trible, Jr. of Virginia, would open commissaries to "former spouses" of military personnel. The third, by far the most expansionist proposal, introduced into the FY 1984 Defense Department appropriations bill by Sen. J. James Exon of Nebraska, would establish a test program for the use of commissary stores by military reservists. This program could bring 950,000 new patrons into the commissary system.

If Congress is ever to exercise cost oversight of the commissary system, it must begin now. New and higher spending patterns have been set in motion. Because the military services build new commissaries from sales proceeds without having to seek construction money from Congress, no oversight has been exercised by Congress either to prevent the emergence of new commissaries in metropolitan areas or to ensure that no duplication of services occurs. In the San Antonio, Tex., metropolitan area, for instance, where five commissaries can be found, two of them are on air force bases (Lackland and Kelly Air Force Base) that literally border one another.

Once new commissaries have been constructed, the House Armed Services Committee has routinely raised commissary appropriations to provide these new stores with employees and inventories. The result of this abdication of congressional oversight has been to make commissary expansion self-perpetuating. With at least another 25 new commissary construction or renovation projects already under way, long-term and ever-higher levels of taxpayer support is once again being committed.

Since FY 1977, the year the last Ford administration proposal for phaseout would have taken effect, at least $3.2 billion in direct appropriated taxpayer costs have been incurred to subsidize commissaries. The indirect, or hidden, costs to the taxpayers in that period, using a calculation developed by DOD for base support and operations utilized in connection with commissaries, run about 42 percent of appropriated costs, or $1.3 billion. The grand total comes to $4.5 billion that could have been saved had Congress acted to place the commissary monopoly on an unprotected competitive footing in the marketplace.

Entirely contracting out the commissaries for operation by the private sector could result in annual savings of up to $758 million. But Congress must first summon the courage to finally define in law the role and goals of a commissary system before it can even begin to confront, and overcome, its own institutional bias for public-sector rather than private-sector solutions.

II. The Agency Structure: How Congress Interferes with Executive Branch Organization

Congress has persistently resisted efforts by the executive branch to streamline and modernize the federal government's organizational structures. This resistance has forced the continuation of operational arrangements that are obsolete, inefficient, and costly, in violation of sound management principles.

The General Accounting Office (GAO), Congress' own investigative agency, has issued numerous reports urging Congress to approve the streamlining of the field structure of the executive agencies. Four reports in particular deserve mention:

- The August 1980 report recommended that the Commerce Department establish consolidated regional field structures for its 21,000 field employees.
- The April 1979 report urged the Agriculture Department to consolidate as many of its 16,970 field offices as possible.
- The April 1978 report encouraged the Department of Housing and Urban Development to consolidate field offices and downgrade other offices with insufficient workloads.
- The October 1978 report suggested that the Customs Service reduce by three the number of regional offices until a six-region structure was achieved.

As will be demonstrated, members of Congress intervened to thwart or delay executive agency attempts to implement each of these four—and many other—GAO recommendations for structural reorganization. Anticipating just this sort of reaction from Congress, the GAO identified, in an August 1980 study ("Streamlining The Federal Field Structure: Potential Opportunities, Barriers, and Actions That Can Be Taken"), how congressional opposition to structural reform is often stimulated. The key players are the government employees directly affected by reorganization.

37

These employees have encouraged congressional intervention, according to the GAO, by using one or more of four tactics:

- They emphasize to members of Congress the human and financial losses likely to occur when an office within their district is closed or consolidated.
- They apply pressure to members of Congress through protest marches, letters, and telephone calls.
- They use alliances between congressional staff and agency personnel who have come to depend on each other for information, advice, and help.
- They enlist the support and influence of former employees of the affected agencies who hold key positions on congressional committees and staffs.

Executive Management: "No Reorganization Without Representation"

Local Weather Stations

> We shall fight them on the beaches. We shall fight them on the landing grounds . . . in the fields and in the streets. We shall fight in the hills. We shall never surrender!

—Winston S. Churchill, 1940

> I am inclined to think, Mr. Secretary, that your bureaucrats pick on this group of stations because they think they have a couple of patsies or suckers in you and me. . . . I will never, ever, give up fighting to keep that weather station, because I know how vital it is.

—Rep. Virginia Smith of Nebraska, 1982

The National Weather Service, which is run by the National Oceanic and Atmospheric Administration (NOAA) of the Commerce Department, includes a field structure of 52 regional weather forecasting offices and 234 local weather service stations. The regional offices, which are staffed 24 hours a day and seven days a week, provide a full range of weather analysis, information, and forecasts. The local offices, many of which are in rural areas and small towns, lack the capacity to do this; instead they adapt forecasts from the regional offices for local use and also provide community liaison.

Officials at NOAA have wanted to restructure the weather service for a number of years to improve services, utilize advanced technology, and eliminate unneeded and obsolete stations. Since 1979 they have been trying to close some of the lowest-priority facilities, the part-time offices with no radar or other equipment. These facilities are not needed for the national forecasting system and provide no information or service that is not readily available from one of the 52 regional offices.

Congress rejected closure proposals for 1979 and 1980, and none were submitted for 1981. In 1982 NOAA tried again, proposing to close 38 of the 234 local weather stations, all with five or fewer employees, for a savings of $1.8 million. All told the closings would affect 85, or 1.5 percent, of the 5,000 jobs in the National Weather Service. Congress agreed to close 18 of the lowest-priority facilities, including the local office at Valentine, Nebr.

Valentine is a community of fewer than 3,000 residents, whose member of Congress since 1974 had been Virginia Smith, a fiscal conservative and a member of the House Appropriations Committee. In 1982 the Valentine weather station was staffed by one employee, whose normal working hours were 9 a.m. to 5 p.m., Monday through Friday.

The weather stations had not yet been closed when, on March 3, 1982, Rep. Smith questioned Secretary of Commerce Malcolm Baldrige about the closing at a hearing of the House Appropriations Subcommittee that has jurisdiction for the Commerce Department, NOAA, and the Weather Service. Even though Congress had agreed to close the 18 weather facilities, Smith was still seeking to keep them open. Her exchange with Baldrige is an illuminating example of how members of Congress seek to control the management process in the executive branch.

Informing Baldrige that she was "fighting to save the Valentine weather station and the 17 other stations marked for dehumanization," Smith said the subject for discussion should be "cutting the real fat out of the budget instead of doing away with these 18 stations." She contended that the "only protection Valentine has from tornadoes is the eyes and judgement of the human beings" assigned to the weather station there. She rejected both of Baldrige's explanations that the Valentine weather station provided no service that was not already available at the regional center in North Platte, Nebr., and that even if North Platte missed a gathering storm, there was no way that Valentine could forecast it.

The commmerce secretary said he did not like closing the weather stations any more than Rep. Smith did, but "where we don't feel they are providing any better service than the public could get from larger, more professional stations, we have to. . . . [I]f you save the dimes, then the dollars add up."

Calling the Commerce Department's research in weather modification a "welfare program for white collar workers," Smith suggested that the agency's budget of $14.4 million for automating local weather service operations be spent instead to keep the 18 part-time stations open. When Baldrige disagreed with this, she urged that public hearings be held on the closures "so that people who are involved and who are paying the taxes would have a voice in the decision." Baldrige responded that if such a process were begun, "It would probably be [the year] 2000 before we got anything done." Noting that the commerce secretary seemed to believe that those 18 facilities already were closed, Smith reminded him that "they are not . . . [and] they ought to be kept open."

She then informed Baldrige that, despite the legislation already adopted to close the 18 weather facilities, she intended to fight to keep them open, saying:

> This is a red-hot issue. The authorizing committees in the House and the Senate are working on it. There is going to be a subcommittee meeting this afternoon. I am not only going to appear before this subcommittee, I am going to appear before the full [Appropriations] Committee.
>
> I am going to appear before the authorizing committee. I am going to present my case when the supplemental budget comes up . . . when any reconciliation or continuing resolution comes up. I am going to fight for it all the way, because I think you are making a ghastly mistake!

Later that year Congress reversed its decision to close the 18 local weather stations and it provided $1.8 million to keep open all 38 stations that NOAA had proposed closing. In 1983 NOAA tried yet again, proposing to close a total of 63 weather service offices, for a savings of $3.8 million. Congress rejected the entire package. No closings have been proposed for 1984. The Valentine weather station is still operating.

National Fish Hatcheries

> *Thousands and millions of unborn fish are clamoring to the Congress today for an opportunity to be hatched at the Tupelo hatchery.*
>
> —Pvt. John Allen, Congressman from Mississippi, Feb. 20, 1901

The Interior Department's Fish and Wildlife Service operates a network of fish hatcheries throughout the nation. The output of these hatcheries is used to restock streams, rivers, ponds, lakes, and other bodies of water, including many that have suffered environmental damage from construction of federal water projects.

As of 1982 there were 89 such hatcheries, including one at Tupelo, Miss., a city of 23,000 located in the northern part of the state. The hatchery opened in 1902, a year after Rep. Allen urged its construction. Tupelo's congressman since 1940 has been Jamie L. Whitten, who currently is chairman of the House Appropriations Committee.

In 1983 the Interior Department proposed to close or transfer to state management 25 fish hatcheries on the grounds that they did "not contribute substantially" to major federal responsibilities in management of the nation's fishery resources. Interior officials further stated that "in large measure the output of these hatcheries has been used to support . . . management of state-owned waters . . . and to stock farm ponds on private lands." Annual cost savings were estimated at $3.3 million, or 12.9 percent of the $25.5 million budget for all national fish hatcheries.

The list of 25 hatcheries included 5 that Interior had proposed for closing in 1982, but which Congress had ordered kept open for one additional year. Among the other 20 were several that also had been proposed for closing in 1982, but which Congress had refused to consider for termination.

This latter group included the hatchery at Tupelo, which Interior officials described as providing 82 percent of the sunfish, catfish, largemouth bass, and walleye it produced for programs involving state-run and privately owned waters. Instead of closing Tupelo in 1982, Congress had acceded to a proposal by Rep. Whitten to rename the facility the Pvt. John Allen National Fish Hatchery in commemoration of the former Mississippi congressman, whose speech on the House floor in 1901 has generally been credited with persuading that body to approve the hatchery there. Tupelo's is the nation's first, and so far only, fish hatchery so honored.

In addition to the operational savings to be gained by closing the group of 20 that included the Tupelo hatchery, Interior officials estimated that another $17 million in unscheduled rehabilitation requirements also would be saved if the hatcheries were shut down or otherwise removed from federal responsibility.

The House Interior Appropriations Subcommittee declined to accept closure of any of the 25 submitted. It even provided funding for the 5 it had previously indicated would remain open only for one additional year. The Senate Interior Appropriations Subcommittee proposed to close 13 of the facilities. In the end, though, Congress closed none of them. As this was being written, 3 of the 25 were in the process of being transferred from federal to state responsibility, and the rest were operating as usual.

Forest Service

Consider what it would be like if you were running a corporation with offices nationwide and your board of directors told you that not only could you never consolidate or close offices to save money but you could also never even *study* the cost savings from reorganization. Now you have a glimpse of the dilemma facing a succession of secretaries of agriculture, who for over ten years have been told by Congress that the Forest Service organizational stucture is sacrosanct and immune to scrutiny.

Through 1971, Agriculture officials had succeeded in closing 8 Forest Service headquarters, thereby reducing the number nationwide from 130 to 122, and in consolidating 124 ranger districts, thereby reducing the number from 775 to 651 nationwide. These economy moves streamlined the management functions while saving the taxpayers millions of dollars.

In 1972, though, the Agriculture Department wanted to reorganize the Forest Service field structure by closing three regional offices located in Utah, Montana, and New Mexico. Consolidation already had proceeded to the point where Agriculture had determined severance pay and the transfer of employees, when Sen. Lee Metcalf of Montana and Sen. Frank E. Moss of Utah intervened, ostensibly on behalf of some Forest Service employees who did not want to be transferred. The two senators inserted language into the Forest Service appropriations bill ordering the Agriculture Department not to spend any money "to change the boundaries of any region, to abolish any region, to move or close any regional office" without the consent of both the House and Senate committees concerned with agriculture and appropriations.

For an agency to obtain the consent of even one committee of Congress for anything is a difficult and time-consuming process, but having four different committees involved, each with veto authority, makes action practically impossible. Each year since 1972 the Agriculture Department has requested removal of the language to permit it to make much-needed alterations in its Forest Service

42

management and organizational structure. Each time the request has fallen on deaf ears.

Sitting on the Senate Agriculture, Nutrition, and Forestry Committee today, each occupying a position on the Soil and Water Conservation Subcommittee, are two of the current senators from Montana and Utah, John Melcher and Orrin G. Hatch.

Below the regional level of administration, this precedent-setting restrictive language also has had a ripple effect. When the Forest Service wanted to consolidate and close the Oconee ranger district in Georgia during 1982, thereby moving the office from Monticello to Eagleton and in the process saving $20,000 a year, Congress once again intervened. At the behest of Sen. Mack Mattingly of Georgia, language was submitted in the House appropriations legislation stating that: "None of the funds contained in the bill should be used to design or construct a new office for the Oconee Ranger District in Georgia. The Forest Service should not proceed with such a project in the future without specific justification and approval by the Committee."

When the administration and the Forest Service attempted to close experimental research laboratories in Bend, Ore., Reno, Nev., and Sewanee, Tenn., Congress intervened to prohibit closure by earmarking funds in excess of $1 million to the three facilities.

HUD Regional Offices

Sen. Robert J. Dole of Kansas reacted quickly and angrily when the Department of Housing and Urban Development (HUD) attempted to transfer most HUD personnel from its Topeka, Kans., office to Kansas City, Mo., as part of a reorganization plan in 1978.

Taking his inspiration from language Congress had adopted a year earlier in requiring the Defense Department to undertake costly studies before reorganizing its base structure, Dole advanced an amendment forcing HUD to study "the impact on the local economy" of any proposed reorganization of a regional area or field office. He directed that all reorganization plans and the cost-benefit studies must be published in the *Federal Register* and then HUD must wait for 90 days, giving Congress an opportunity to react. "The language . . . will keep HUD bureaucrats from transferring personnel or functions out of existing HUD field offices," Dole explained in remarks on the Senate floor.

Sen. William Proxmire of Wisconsin questioned the wisdom of forcing HUD to undertake studies of the impact on the local economy of even minor office changes: "It would be very, very hard to estimate the effect of a move of a headquarters on the local tax base. . . . I am not sure which local economy he [Dole] might be referring to. . . ."

Replied Sen. Dole:

> I would say that the local economy referred to is the one in which the HUD office is located. . . . Mr. President, this reorganization is disrupting the lives of countless HUD employees. . . . [With] section 712 in place, and with the legislative history that has been made on the floor to protect existing HUD offices—our offices should be safe.

Apparently moved by Sen. Dole's concerns, Sen. Proxmire agreed to the amendment on behalf of his party, and the amendment was placed into law.

Other Examples of Micromanagement

Example No. 1. The Agriculture Department wanted to close down 27 area offices of the Food Safety and Inspection Service that were no longer needed, as well as the Fort Worth, Tex., training center, at an annual cost saving of $2.5 million. However, Rep. Jack E. Hightower of Texas, a member of the Agricultural Appropriations Subcommittee, in 1982 stepped in to save the Forth Worth training center and with it the 27 offices.

Example No. 2. In 1982 the state director of the Farmers Home Administration recommended reducing the offices in Oklahoma's Love and Coal counties to part-time status because business was so slow. They would be open just one day a week. The recommendation, made in January 1982, worked its way up the line and was approved by the FmHA administrator in May. Those offices were in two of the seventeen counties that form Oklahoma's Third Congressional District, which is represented by Wesley W. Watkins, a member of the House Agricultural Appropriations Subcommittee. The committee report that year directed Agriculture Department officials to "maintain full-service county offices with normal operating hours in Love County and Coal County, Oklahoma."

The agency modified its plans so that the offices were open five days a week with full-time clerical staff and with professional staff on hand one day a week. That was not good enough, though. For the 1984 fiscal year the agency was directed to "maintain full-service loan offices," along with the clerical staff.

Example No. 3. The Agricultural Research Service (ARS) wanted to close two stations in Florida: Belle Glade and Lake Alfred. In response Sen. Lawton Chiles of Florida, a member of the Appropriations Committee, got language added to the 1984 spending bill directing ARS to keep those offices open and staffed.

Example No. 4. If the impression is growing that no item is too small for the world's greatest deliberative body to overlook, consider the ARS's plan to shift research on barley from Brookings, S.D., to focus on more fundamental research elsewhere. Just $90,000 was involved. Nevertheless that was enough to get Sen. James Abdnor of South Dakota, a member of the Agricultural Appropriations Subcommittee, to add language to the subcommittee's report for the 1984 money bill saying that while the need for basic research in barley is supported, $90,000 is going to stay at Brookings.

Example No. 5. In 1981 the Soil Conservation Service wanted to put a hold on new starts of erosion and flood-control projects while those in the works underwent a review by the Water Resources Council. Two executive orders to that effect were issued by the president. Congressional response was to increase funding for watershed and flood-prevention operations by 50 percent over administration requests, from $128.5 million to $192.5 million. In the process Sen. Robert C. Byrd of West Virginia persuaded his colleagues to amend the statute authorizing this program so as to exempt permanently six watershed projects from the Water Resources Council's review. Two were in his state; the others were in Kansas, Kentucky, Missouri, and New York. Since then Congress has directed the agency to add 50 more new projects to its list and has increased total funding by 55 percent over administration requests, for a total of $579.5 million through FY 1983.

Example No. 6. The Department of Interior wanted to consolidate its twelve Bureau of Indian Affairs area offices, which administer programs on a regionwide basis, into five regional service centers and two special services offices. Estimated savings to taxpayers would have been $16 million annually. Rep. Sidney R. Yates of Illinois, chairman of the Interior Appropriations Subcommittee, has thwarted this consolidation attempt by repeatedly raising new questions that challenge most aspects of the character and motivation of this reorganization.

Example No. 7. Sen. Dennis DeConcini of Arizona led a group of his colleagues in adding language to the Treasury Department appropriations bill to prevent any expenditure of funds "to reduce the number of Customs Service regions below seven during fiscal year 1984." The language also required that both House and Senate appropriations committees be notified in writing six months in advance of any proposed "closure by consolidation of Customs facilities or proposed reduction or transfer of personnel."

Example No. 8. The Department of Labor has considered over the past two years a reduction in the number of field stations handling black lung benefit claims, owing to a sharply decreasing workload. At least 20 such stations were under consideration for closure, at an annual savings of $6,000 each, or $120,000 total. Before Labor could even submit such a proposal with a justification and projected cost savings, Sen. Byrd of West Virginia inserted language into the department's FY 1983 budget directing "that the Department of Labor take no action to close black lung field offices."

Example No. 9. The General Services Administration (GSA) wanted to close its Federal Information Center office in Sacramento, Calif., with three employees in 1981, and channel requests for government information through a toll-free telephone hot line. But a letter-writing campaign by California senators Alan Cranston and Pete Wilson, along with representatives Norman D. Shumway, Robert T. Matsui, Victor Fazio, and Gene Chappie, intimidated the GSA into suspending its cost-cutting plan.

Example No. 10. During the Carter years the State Department closed for budgetary reasons seven consulates in Italy, Austria, Sweden, West Germany, France, Burma, and Australia. Sen. Claiborne Pell of Rhode Island and Rep. Clement J. Zablocki of Wisconsin, chairman of the House Foreign Affairs Committee, decided they wanted the consulates reopened despite State Department assurances that it could get along without them. Pell and Zablocki inserted legislative language, beginning in FY 1982, directing that $400,000 of State Department funds be reprogrammed to open the seven consulates, saying that until this was accomplished, no new consulates could be opened by the State Department anywhere in the world. The actual cost to taxpayers for reopening the consulates came to over $1 million, as the building in Bremen, West Germany, had already been sold and a new consulate site had to be acquired.

Example No. 11. The Interior Department's Office of Surface Mining wanted to handle projects of its Rural Abandoned Mine Program through a state grant mechanism that would eliminate a layer of bureaucracy at the Soil Conservation Service of the Agriculture Department, where the program money is sent for disbursement. The savings were estimated at $650,000 annually. Rep. Ralph S. Regula of Ohio inserted language in the FY 1984 appropriations bill to prevent this direct funding to the states.

Example No. 12. Regional Information Sharing System (RISS) programs were a state and local concept of enabling state and local jurisdictions to share intelligence information concerning criminal activity. Funding had been provided by the Law Enforcement Assistance Administration until that agency had been disbanded several years ago. The Justice Department concluded that if the program were worthwhile, state and local governments should be willing to help pay for it. They have not been, so Justice opposed assuming the entire financial burden. Sen. Paul Laxalt of Nevada inserted language into the FY 1984 Justice Department appropriations bill to force the agency to spend $9.9 million on seven regional information programs.

Example No. 13. In a burst of micromanaging language that had baffled officials of the Treasury Department, Rep. Victor Fazio of California and Sen. James Abdnor of South Dakota oversaw insertion into the FY 1984 Treasury Department appropriations bill the following: "None of the funds made available to the Department of the Treasury by this Act or any other Act shall be used to implement changes shortening the time granted, or altering the mode of payment and receipt, or use of lock boxes for payment of excise taxes by law or regulations in effect on January 1, 1981."

Micromanaging Property Disposal

The federal government owns one-third of the total land area of the United States, which makes it the nation's largest tenant, landlord, and holder of grazing land and timberland. Sale of only 0.5 percent of this federal property would generate at least $900 million in revenue over three years. Under the Reagan administration's land-sales program, the General Services Administration (GSA) was supposed to raise $9 billion over five years by selling commercial, residential, and industrial properties deemed by the government to be no longer necessary holdings or too costly to maintain. Another $8 billion was to have been raised through the sale of public land held by the Agriculture and Interior departments.

Congress intervened on several different levels to thwart these goals. Led by Rep. Daniel K. Akaka of Hawaii, the House refused to fund for FY 1985 the White House Property Review Board, which was to have made property sale determinations. Rep. Akaka got involved when the review board recommended selling off part of Fort DeRussy, a military recreation complex on Waikiki Beach in Hawaii.

While preserving the status quo of federal ownership on one level, members of Congress have been diligently undermining the property sales program from another angle as well; they have been drafting legislation to force the executive branch to turn over these properties at no cost to state and local governments. Here are eleven representative pieces of legislation introduced during the 98th Congress to prohibit the sale of federal property or force such transfers at no cost:

- S. 423 and H.R. 1688, introduced by Sen. Charles McC. Mathias, Jr. and Rep. Steny H. Hoyer of Maryland, would prohibit the sale, conveyance, or lease of a portion of the Beltsville Agricultural Research Center, Greenbelt, Md.
- H.R. 1165, introduced by Rep. Marilyn L. Lloyd of Tennessee, would prohibit the disposal of 12.5 acres of surplus land adjacent to the Federal Building located in Oak Ridge, Tenn.
- H.R. 1985, introduced by Rep. Ike F. Andrews of North Carolina, would prohibit the sale of certain lands located in Research Triangle Park, N.C.
- H.R. 2869, introduced by Rep. Cecil Heftel of Hawaii, would provide for the conveyance of certain federal property located in Hawaii to the state of Hawaii.
- H.R. 1002, introduced by Rep. Chalmers P. Wylie of Ohio, would direct the secretary of the army to convey to the state of Ohio, without monetary consideration, approximately 834.09 acres of land.
- H.R. 1962, introduced by Rep. Ronnie G. Flippo of Alabama, would authorize the secretary of the army to convey to the Alabama Space Science Exhibit Commission, without monetary consideration, all right, title, and interest in approximately 65 acres of land located in Redstone Arsenal.

- H.R. 3305 and S. 1472, introduced by Rep. James H. Scheuer and Sen. Daniel P. Moynihan, both of New York, would require the disposal of certain lands at Fort Totten, N.Y., for public health and park and recreation purposes.
- S. 507, introduced by Sen. Paul D. Laxalt of Nevada, would authorize the secretary of the army to convey to the county of Mineral, Nev., without monetary consideration, approximately 237.52 acres of land within the Hawthorne Army Ammunition Plant.
- S. 1122, introduced by Sen. James R. Sasser of Tennessee, authorizes the conveyance to the city of Clarksville, the county of Montgomery, and the county of Stewart in Tennessee, without monetary consideration, all right, title, and interest in approximately 208.49 acres of land located in Montgomery County, Tenn.

The Government Printing Office: "You Can't Run an Efficient Business with a Legislative Body"

Three blocks from the U.S. Capitol sits a 19th-century, eight-story red brick building containing 36 acres of floor space and some 70 printing presses. It is the Government Printing Office (GPO). As mandated by Congress in 1860, it publishes the *Congressional Record*, the *Federal Register*, and copies of hearings and legislation, and it serves as the printing procurement officer for executive branch agencies. Even though the GPO is the largest arm of the legislative branch with nearly 6,000 employees, its chief executive officer— the public printer—is appointed by the president. This delicate relationship has been strained as Congress in recent years has pursued an aggressive and expansive policy of micromanaging the printing needs of the entire federal government.

The agent of that activism has been GPO's overseer, the Joint Committee on Printing (JCP), composed of ten members of Congress—five from the Senate Rules and Administration Committee and five from the House Administration Committee. Rarely has the JCP met twice in a year, preferring instead to delegate its oversight responsibility to an 18-member staff. Congressional turnover on the committee is high. Most members vote by proxy and only a few have ever ventured the ten-minute walk to even visit the GPO facilities. To put it bluntly, members of the JCP historically have regarded their assignment as a low or unimportant legislative priority.

By default, power within the JCP has come to be vested in its chairman and vice-chairman, who in turn hire the staff director and other important personnel to make the everyday decisions affecting the entire federal government printing structure. Enactment of Title 44 of the U.S. Code in 1895 endowed the JCP with statutory oversight of executive agency printing. But it is a series of regulations promulgated by the JCP right up until the present day that has extended the JCP's grip into every area of agency operations, including the most microscopic of bureaucratic details.

The JCP has given itself veto authority over all editorial, marketing, and pricing decisions of the agencies that involve printing. Approval must be sought from the JCP for the purchase of printing-related equipment, for the size and quality of paper to be used, for the printing processes and range of colors, as well as the design and format of everything printed on paper.

Some examples of this micromanaging border on the absurd. For instance the JCP has given itself the right to approve or disapprove the "style, size and format" of calendars supplied to hang on the walls of agency offices. The JCP also demands the right to approve "all stationery with preprinted mastheads" that include the names of officers or officials of both the executive and judicial branches of government.

When an agency wants to contract out for a printing job, it must allow the GPO to negotiate and administer the contract. This procurement power was endowed by the JCP in 1965. Such regulations have brought numerous nonprinting areas of the executive branch effectively under JCP control as well. Electrostatic reproduction and agency user charges for publications are merely two examples of such areas.

This progressive intrusion into executive agency operations by a congressional joint committee that has assumed the functions of a regulatory body poses a serious institutional conflict for the future. Just such a prediction was made implicitly in 1979 by an official of the GAO in testimony before two congressional committees. Werner Grosshans, associate director of the GAO's Logistics and Communications Division, described the relationship between the JCP and the agencies as conforming neither to "prudent business practice" nor to "normal Government practices from the standpoint of separation of powers between the Executive and Legislative branches. . . ." Strictly from an organizational perspective, said Grosshans, "today's printing structure is inappropriate."

Comprehensive legislation was introduced in 1979 to revise Title 44 and reorganize the federal government's printing structure. Offered by the JCP chairman and vice-chairman, Sen. Claiborne Pell of Rhode Island and Rep. Frank Thompson, Jr. of New Jersey, the bill would have established a board of directors, appointed by the president and confirmed by the Senate, to replace the JCP. This board would select the public printer and carry on the regulations previously implemented by the JCP.

"If it is the desire of the Congress to abolish the Joint Committee on Printing," said Public Printer John Boyle in testimony on the bill, "and again I say that I can understand the dissatisfaction of the Members with the administrative and operational duties they are faced with, then why not consider transferring all of the present functions of the Joint Committee on Printing to the Government Printing Office, together with the remedial powers necessary to enforce the regulations, by making the Government Printing Office an independent agency in the Legislative Branch of Government?"

Testified William Boarman, president of GPO's typographical union: "The Joint Committee on Printing [has become] a court of last resort, frequently being dragged into operational problems at the worst possible time in the legislative process, when other congressional demands are more pressing. Plain and simple, the GPO is a business, and you can't run a business with a legislative body."

These and a wide variety of other comments on the proposed restructuring accumulated to reflect as well the divisions within Congress, where no consensus for change of any sort could be reached. After four days of hearings on the bill in July 1979, nothing happened. Congress could not even decide to rid itself of a committee and a role that none of its members seemed to want.

The more micromanaging the JCP has exercised over agency administrative functions, the less attention it has paid to oversight of the costs associated with these decisions. When attempts have been made, without the JCP's initiative, to rectify organizational or management problems that have resulted in an outpouring of tax- payers' dollars, the JCP has often reacted jealously and defiantly.

A case in point is Public Printer Danford Sawyer's attempt to close or consolidate 23 of GPO's 27 regional bookstores. In 1981 the bookstores, where government publications are purchased or ordered, lost $9.7 million. Most of the stores are in hidden and inaccessible locations in large cities. The Chicago outlet, for instance, can be found, if you know where to look, on the 13th floor of a downtown federal building. Sawyer wanted to close or consolidate the stores because "there's absolutely no need for them; ninety-two percent of our publications were sold by direct mail anyway."

Employees of the 27 bookstores—two or three people are employed by each store—bombarded members of the JCP with letters and petitions demanding that the facilities be kept open. JCP chairman Sen. Mathias of Maryland, in whose state nearly half of all GPO employees reside, and the vice-chairman, Rep. Augustus F. Hawkins of California, called a special committee meeting and persuaded the JCP to pass a resolution rejecting any change in the bookstore status quo, along with preventing Sawyer from attempting other personnel changes designed to cut costs.

There was a time in the not-too-distant past when Congress applauded rather than condemned public printers who took the initiative to save the taxpayers money. Back in 1955 Public Printer Raymond Blattenberger reduced the GPO payroll by 800 employees, instituted a series of cost-control measures, and returned $11 million to the public treasury (about $41 million in current dollars). He said his guiding principle was simple—to run the GPO as he had his own private printing business, as efficiently and cost-effectively as possible. Congress rewarded him with letters of praise, speeches, and commendations.

Somewhere along the way the attitude of Congress toward costs has changed. Nowhere is this more evident than in the way Congress, through the JCP, has treated GPO's nearly 6,000 employees.

GPO's 18 unions bargain collectively with the public printer and the JCP, whereas most other federal workers have their wages set under the federal wage system of the Civil Service Commission. The by-product of this preferential wage-setting system has been an escalation of GPO salaries far beyond those of other federal employees. The most dramatic increases occurred during the 1970s, when the JCP chairmanship and vice-chairmanship rotated between Sen. Howard W. Cannon of Nevada, Rep. Wayne L. Hays of Ohio, Sen. Claiborne Pell of Rhode Island, and Rep. Frank Thompson, Jr. of New Jersey. Salaries increased 14.9 percent in 1971, 7 percent in 1972, 8.4 percent in 1973, 12.1 percent in 1974, and 10.4 percent in 1975, for a cumulative total of 64.9 percent over the five years. By contrast other federal employees received only a 29.8 percent cumulative salary increase over the same five-year period.

A GAO report in 1976 sharply criticized the JCP's benevolence with tax money:

> The Government should not pay less than other employers, but it cannot afford to be a more generous employer than the industries that support it with their taxes. . . . We believe that GPO pay rates should follow wage movements in the private sector and that GPO should not be a wage leader.

This GAO report went on to recommend that GPO employees be brought under the federal wage system and be paid and classified the same as other federal workers. But Congress did not respond to these suggestions.

An October 1981 study by the Department of Defense's wage-fixing authority found that GPO wages in all 23 job categories it studied were significantly higher than those of other government workers. A GPO painter, for instance, received $14.35 an hour, while the average for other government agency painters was only $10.76 an hour. GAO did a second review of pay inequities in May 1982 by comparing six occupations at GPO to similar occupations elsewhere in the federal government. The wage differential held. GPO carpenters were found to be making 28.8 percent more than other government carpenters; GPO electricians were making 22.4 percent more than other federal electricians.

Public Printer Danford Sawyer compiled statistics from a nationwide survey to compute an 11-city wage average for the printing industry. In every job category studied, the GPO wages far exceeded those of the private sector: GPO pressmen received $17.53 an hour compared to $13.33 for the private sector; GPO bookbinders received $16.68 an hour compared to $12.77 an hour for industry.

Union officials and the JCP staff complained that these wage comparisons were not an accurate reflection because they failed to take into account the unique character of duties performed by GPO workers. To answer that criticism, GAO undertook yet a third study of the GPO wage structure in early 1983. It compared 21 GPO job categories to similar positions in the agencies. Not only did GAO find the job duties to be comparable, it discovered that in many instances the higher-paid GPO employees were actually doing less-demanding work than their counterparts in other agencies. "The wage difference between GPO employees and other Federal employees for calendar year 1982," noted the GAO, "averaged 42 percent overall, or $8,410—a range of $3,222 to $17,879 ($1.55 to

$8.59 an hour) more than the representative General Schedule or FWS wage rate for similar occupations."

Some of the pay differences for certain job classifications are simply astounding. The GAO found, for instance, that a journeyman GPO proofreader earns $30,252 annually, while proofreaders at executive agencies receive an average salary of $12,473—a wage disparity of 143 percent.

Just as the JCP has allowed the wages of its printing employees to spiral out of control, so has it failed to control and monitor the proliferation of printing plants operated by the various federal agencies. Using a waiver process, a government agency can petition the JCP for a charter to buy and operate its own printing facilities. By the summer of 1981 over 300 such plants were in place, 50 of them in the Washington, D.C., area, some within a few blocks of the GPO itself. A GAO study of the plants found that some operated at costs 16 times higher than those in the private sector. The costs just in the D.C. area ranged from $8.28 per thousand production units at the U.S. Army's Fort Belvoir facility to over $64 per thousand at a nearby U.S. Navy plant. The JCP had never done an analysis of why such wide variations occurred; nor had it proposed solutions to lower these costs.

It was difficult to determine if federal printing was being done economically governmentwide, the GAO concluded, because the JCP had "only loosely monitored" personnel, plant, and press capacities. The amount of commercially procurable work being done in-house at these plants was also "not known" and could be as high as 23 percent of all printing, again because the JCP had not made it a policy to monitor costs closely.

The GAO urged a systemwide consolidation of these plants that JCP had allowed to proliferate, with every existing agency printing facility to be subjected to a rejustification process. Said the GAO: "The agencies should also certify that they have considered other options, such as interagency support, and that they have selected the least costly viable option."

Furthermore, added the GAO, the JCP should develop, in cooperation with the Office of Management and Budget (OMB), a long-range plan to ensure "effective service at reasonable cost." Public Printer Danford Sawyer estimated that consolidating or closing most of these JCP-approved plants would save the taxpayers at least $70 million annually.

In a memorandum, Sawyer endorsed GAO's recommendation of

a joint JCP-OMB rejustification, since it was clear to him that Congress could "no longer sit idly by and let such neglect, delay, duplication and waste continue." But JCP's chairman, Sen. Mathias, bridled at the idea of having OMB, an executive agency, in his words "looking over our shoulder." Sen. Wendell H. Ford of Kentucky also resisted the idea, telling other JCP members in a committee session, "as long as we can keep OMB out, the better off we are going to be."

Instead of the comprehensive review that Sawyer and the GAO wanted of all government printing plants, the JCP approved only a pilot study of facilities in New York City. When even this limited study came back with recommendations for the closure of nearly all the New York plants examined, pressure for a nationwide rejustification mounted.

In early 1983, OMB, having historically paid little attention to government printing or related costs, now saw the duplication of effort and waste as requiring its oversight. It initiated a rejustification program designed to identify needless plants while shifting more printing and duplicating work from the government to the private sector.

Initial information gathered by OMB indicates that of the 950 executive branch printing and duplicating facilities it has identified worldwide, according to OMB Deputy Director Joseph R. Wright, Jr., "The majority of those facilities are producing routine printing at a cost to the taxpayer of more than three times that charged by commercial printers now on contract to the Government Printing Office." The majority of the presses in use were found to be operating at "less than 35 percent of capability." OMB has compiled recommendations for over 130 plant closures that, if enacted, are expected to save at least $30 million yearly.

A potential stumbling block to any nationwide realignment of printing plants is of course the JCP, which claims that because it authorized the plants in the first place, only it can deauthorize, consolidate, or close them. When OMB officials held a press conference to announce proposed plant closures, no representative of the JCP made an appearance. The next day's *Washington Post* (November 2, 1983) carried the following: "But a committee [JCP] aide later suggested that the closing might meet with less than unbridled enthusiasm on Capitol Hill. 'You didn't see the joint committee there at the news conference did you?' said committee aide Faye Padgett."

If OMB chooses to exercise purse-string authority and simply deny the agencies funding for affected printing plants, and the JCP resists, then similar kinds of thorny constitutional questions over separation of powers that already characterize the JCP/GPO relationship may soon arise in a more volatile political environment.

In other areas as well, JCP actions may provoke conflict. Proposed new regulations prepared by the JCP staff contain language extending JCP control for the first time over all executive agency electronic transmissions of information. This may place the JCP on another collision course with the executive branch.

Along with the cost of other legislative branch operations, Congress has allowed GPO personnel costs to skyrocket and government printing plants to proliferate without a cost-conscious growth plan. Then, claiming an oversight role, it has enacted regulations that micromanage in almost absurd detail the printing needs of the executive branch, again irrespective of the costs. Is it any wonder that at least one cost-concerned segment of government has seen the need to "look over Congress' shoulder"?

III. The Agency Systems: How Congress Meddles with Executive Branch Operations

Sound management of an organization requires a system for utilizing the structure that has been created to carry out the established mission. If a system is defined as a set of principles, rules, or laws designed to govern the actions of individuals in pursuit of their designated organizational responsibilities, there is no question that Congress, as it writes legislation, is deeply involved in the practice of formulating systems for the executive branch.

This is considerably beyond the role of setting basic goals and policies that is usually found among boards of directors or other groups whose principal function is to "set the rules," to make policy rather than implement it. A basic principle of sound management is that established rules and procedures should be set aside or waived only in exceptional circumstances, and certainly not to benefit friends or associates of those who set the rules. Unfortunately, in addition to writing the rules, Congress all too often then turns around and makes exceptions to them, usually in order to exercise the very kind of favoritism the rules were written to prevent in the first place. Raising costs to taxpayers and making demands upon programs that they were not designed to meet are just a few of the harmful effects of these practices on the executive branch and the nation as a whole, as the following examples demonstrate.

Program Rules: "Making Exceptions for Friends"

Metal Stockpiling

Metals considered necessary to national defense are stockpiled after being purchased with funds from the National Defense Stockpile Transaction Fund, which is administered by the General Services Administration (GSA). Authority for determining which metals are strategic and the quantity of each to be acquired is given to the president by the Stock Piling Act. This act states that the purpose of the stockpile "is to serve the interest of national defense only and is not to be used for economic or budgetary purposes."

In FY 1981 Sen. James A. McClure of Idaho, chairman of the Energy and Natural Resources Committee, inserted a rider to the Defense Appropriation Act effectively preventing GSA from selling any silver from its stockpile until the president had determined it was excess and until Congress had given its "prior approval [to] the recommended method of disposal." The president was given a deadline to respond, July 1, 1982; after that date, according to a GSA legal analysis, the moratorium on selling silver would become permanent. Responsibility for responding to the deadline on behalf of the president was vested in the Cabinet Council on Natural Resources, chaired by the secretary of interior. To date the council has not responded.

The Congressional Budget Office (CBO) prepared a study in FY 1981 estimating the federal silver inventory at 139.5 million troy ounces valued at $2.1 billion. Sale of the excess, which GSA had estimated at 105 million troy ounces by FY 1984, could produce a minor windfall for the public treasury. But, as the CBO further pointed out, "to the extent that disposal might lower silver prices, the legislation [to allow disposal] would be opposed by domestic mining and metal processing industries." In the case of Sen. McClure, for example, his home state of Idaho is one of the nation's principal metals mining states.

Two other pieces of legislation pending before Congress would further hamstring GSA's and the president's ability to administer the metals stockpile based on strategic rather than parochial considerations. Four mining state senators—Dennis DeConcini of Arizona, Jeff Bingaman and Pete V. Domenici of New Mexico, and John Melcher of Montana—have submitted a bill to force GSA to purchase from domestic producers at least 200,000 short tons of copper valued at $300 million for the National Defense Stockpile. Similar legislation has been introduced in the House by Reps. Morris K. Udall and James McNulty of Arizona. It directs the GSA to acquire within one year $85 million of domestic copper using the National Defense Stockpile Transaction Fund.

GSA officials have responded:

> At the present time and operating within the mandate of the Stock Piling act, acquiring $300 million of copper is a practical impossibility without direct appropriations. Currently, and in the fore-

seeable future, there will not be sufficient funds to finance such an acquisition.

Because the stockpile operates on a revolving fund, one of the reasons there is insufficient funding to buy the copper is directly attributable to the legislative constraint on GSA's selling any stockpiled silver to raise the needed capital.

GSA further opposes these bills because they blatantly violate provisions of the Stock Piling Act, which stipulates that the stockpile cannot be used to subsidize affected industries. In GSA's words:

> We are cognizant of the fact that both demand and prices for copper have fallen. This situation is not unique to the domestic copper mining industry. However, GSA believes it is inappropriate to use moneys in the Fund as a means to ameliorate economic conditions in a particular industry.
>
> We also believe it to be inappropriate and contrary to the Stock Piling Act for Congress to establish priorities on the expenditure of Stockpile moneys on an ad hoc basis for reasons unrelated to the Stockpile program. The authority for determining which materials are strategic and critical and the quantity to be acquired is vested in the President by the Stock Piling Act.

Federal Power Marketing Administrations

Congress is so sensitive to questions about the pricing of federally produced hydroelectric power sold to the public that it has prohibited the executive branch from not only studying the matter but also even discussing it.

The concept of federal hydroelectric power developed early in the 20th century as the government undertook the construction and operation of dams and reservoirs across the nation. The idea was for the federal government to invest in power-generating capacity beyond that required to operate the facilities and to sell this excess power to benefit local consumers. The revenues from the sales were supposed to repay the government for its investment and for the costs of producing this excess power.

There are six federal power marketing administrations (PMAs). They are the Tennessee Valley Authority (TVA), the Southeastern PMA, the Southwestern PMA, the Western Area PMA, the Bonneville (Pacific Northwest) PMA, and the Alaska PMA. Together the six cover 38 of the 50 states, with only New England and portions of the Upper Midwest not included in this network. The TVA, a separate federal entity, accounted for 5.8 percent of all U.S. electric production in FY 1982, according to the PPSSCC Task Force on Privatization. The other five PMAs, which are part of the Department of Energy, accounted for 6 percent in FY 1982.

While TVA owns and operates the facilities that produce the electricity it markets, such is not the case for the other five PMAs. They buy the power produced by dams owned by the Interior Department or the U.S. Army Corps of Engineers and then use transmission lines to transport it to customers.

The rates the PMAs charge for this power are set at levels determined by studies designed to show that the revenues will be adequate to repay the federal government its investment, plus interest, over 50 years. These studies are prepared by the PMA staffs, reviewed by the Department of Energy, and then approved or disapproved by the Federal Energy Regulatory Commission. The PPSSCC Task Force on Energy reported that in FY 1981 the wholesale rate PMAs charged to local utilities averaged less than half the rule-of-thumb figure for U.S. hydropower and only one-third the wholesale rate for electricity charged by nonfederal utilities during calendar year 1980.

In the past, Congress has expressed concern that the rates charged be adequate to meet the repayment obligations. The House Appropriations Subcommittee for Energy and Water Development, in the report accompanying its FY 1983 spending bill, said it continued to have "concerns that the power marketing administrations have not been charging rates sufficient to repay their obligations under the law."

At a hearing before this subcommittee on February 24, 1983, as preparations began for the FY 1983 appropriations measure, Robert L. McPhail, administrator of the Western Area PMA, stated that, in carrying out their functions, the PMAs are required to "develop rates adequate to repay the Federal investment with interest." At the same hearing, Richard B. Risk, Jr., administrator of the Southwestern PMA, said the mission of his agency was to "encourage the most widespread use of power at the lowest possible rates to consumers consistent with sound business principles."

As of 1982 the federal government had a total capital investment of $12.8 billion in the five PMAs (excluding TVA), of which $2.8 billion had been repaid. Despite revenues estimated by the Energy Department at $2.8 billion for FY 1983 and $3.5 billion for FY 1984, Congress has continued to vote taxpayer subsidies for the PMAs, in the sum of $249.2 million in 1983.

In 1982 a working group was organized under the leadership of the president's Council of Economic Advisers to explore the adequacy of rate and access policy of the federal power marketing entities. The group's first organizational meeting was held on July 29 of that year. Within two months, though, Congress moved to squelch the group. On September 24, nine members of Congress, all from the Pacific Northwest, signed a letter to the president expressing "deep concern" that the proposed study of federal power rate-making policies posed a "fundamental threat to the concept of public power and to the economy of the Pacific Northwest." Five days later, on September 29, Sen. James A. McClure of Idaho and Sen. James R. Sasser of Tennessee offered an amendment to the Continuing Appropriations Resolution for FY 1983. Their amendment was to prohibit the use of any funds for the purpose of conducting "any studies relating to or leading to the possibility of changing from the currently required 'at cost' to a 'market rate' method for the pricing of hydroelectric power" by the PMAs.

The possibility of even broaching the subject had been choked off, as members of a PPSSCC task force discovered during the summer of 1983, when they sought to interview officials at the Office of Management and Budget (OMB) about the aborted rate-making study. OMB officials told the task force members they would not even discuss the subject, because doing so would constitute a forbidden expenditure of federal funds, in the form of the salaries they would be paid during the time they would be taking to discuss the matter.

To ensure that any questioning of rate-making policies by the PMAs remains strictly off limits to the executive branch, Sen. Mark O. Hatfield of Oregon, chairman of the Senate Appropriations Committee, added the McClure-Sasser language to the FY 1984 energy and water appropriations bill. Thus it remains in law.

Canceling Local Liabilities

In December 1978, about the time Rep. Jamie L. Whitten of Mississippi was being elevated by his colleagues to be chairman of the House Appropriations Committee, two other Mississippi politicians were being found guilty of conspiring to defraud the federal government. One was Bill Burgin, then chairman of the Mississippi Senate Appropriations Committee and considered one of the state's most powerful figures. The other was Flavous Lambert, a former state senator. They were convicted, fined $10,000 each, and sentenced to prison terms for taking kickbacks from two federally funded Head Start contracts totaling $860,000.

The contracts, with the Mississippi Department of Public Welfare, were for a program to work with 1,600 children in Mississippi Head Start centers. The trial and conviction resulted from indictments that followed a four-month investigation by the Federal Bureau of Investigation and the inspector general of the Department of Health and Human Services (HHS).

Lambert, according to trial evidence, received about $354,000 as a kickback from the contractor; Burgin received $96,000 of that from Lambert, ostensibly to pay off legal debts. Because 75 percent of the contracts, or about $645,000 involved federal dollars, a question arose as to whether Mississippi owed HHS a refund of some of the money, in that kickbacks are not considered an appropriate expenditure of taxpayer dollars.

About the same time, federal investigators also were looking at yet another Mississippi Head Start contract involving a different group. This one was for $336,000. This probe also led to court action resulting in fines and orders to make restitution. For the next three years, until the end of 1981, Mississippi and HHS officials wrangled back and forth over whether, and how much, the state owed Washington in refunds for the federal portion of the misspent money.

Finally, in November, 1981, Mississippi Governor William Winter formally requested that the state not be held liable for making good on the misspent funds. HHS Secretary Richard S. Schweiker responded by calling in the department's inspector general to review the cases. Following an audit that ran from January to July of 1982, the HHS inspector general concluded that in both sets of contracts wildly inflated claims of services had been made in support of the invoices submitted, and that the Mississippi Department of Public Welfare had exercised inadequate control over the financial aspects of the projects. As one example, the auditors said, a psychologist would have had to work 239 hours in five days to perform the services for which bills were submitted and paid. In two reports, both dated December 21, 1982, the HHS inspector general concluded that Mississippi owed HHS a total of $468,216, based on audits of the two different sets of contracts.

HHS funnels enormous amounts of federal dollars each year to the states for social services programs. Because the system is so huge and complex, initial payments for each year are made on the basis of estimated requirements. The states and HHS later settle their accounts on the basis of actual disbursements. Rather than demand a refund from Mississippi, HHS normally would have simply reduced the next year's allotment for the state.

That will not happen in this case, however. Buried in the massive jobs bill that was enacted on March 24, 1983, is a paragraph inserted by Rep. Whitten that has a special meaning to the state of Mississippi. Tacked onto a section that adds $225 million to the social services block grant for day care and other needs, it says simply that "the State allotment for fiscal year 1983 shall not be reduced to offset any reduction in a prior year allotment made pursuant to the Department of Health and Human Services, OIG control number 030550 and 030551." Those are the control numbers for the two HHS inspector general audits that grew out of those Mississippi contracts, for which one state senator drew a 15-month jail term and the other was sentenced to two years.

One of the strongest arguments favored by supporters of public works projects, such as water and power facilities, is that the users repay the federal government at least part of the construction costs. In fact, it is the law.

Congress can change the law, but often finds it easier to write a directive into a committee report. While such a report is not considered as completely binding on an agency, executive branch officials generally treat report language as orders to be followed. Sometimes, however, the directive in the report will conflict with an existing statute. The Dickinson Dam may be a case in point.

Dickinson, N.D., a community of 15,000 on the Heart River, gets its water from a dam and reservoir built by the Bureau of Reclamation in 1950. In 1976 Congress authorized modification of the dam to increase water-storage capacity by installing a special gate on the existing spillway. A contract was written whereby the bureau would build the gate and the city would repay the costs. City commissioners also had the right to reject or accept the construction bid.

All went well until September 1980, five months after the city had approved the design and construction contract. A newly hired consulting engineer for Dickinson raised questions about the design of the gate. Work stopped while the city went back to the drawing boards. Subsequently, though, federal officials told the city officials that their new plan would not work, and added that if Dickinson found the original design totally unacceptable, the only option was to terminate the contract and start all over. It would delay work about two years.

Six weeks later, in early January 1981, Dickinson told the Bureau of Reclamation to move as fast as possible to finish the project following the original design. By February 1982, it was about complete and was deemed ready to be placed in service. After two weeks of operation, the gate failed. Subsequent tests showed that the manufacturer's design was inadequate, and the prime contractor was told to correct the problem. A number of safety measures also were added, such as a deicing system and a boom to keep large chunks of ice from flowing over the gate and down the spillway.

Under the contract Dickinson was responsible for the operation and maintenance of the new system, but the delays and changes had driven the annual cost from the $6,000 estimated in 1975 to $10,000 in 1983. Under the circumstances, the city did not want to assume the responsibility and cost of operating and maintaining the modified dam; it wanted the Bureau of Reclamation to do so. However, the position of the bureau was that, under the law, it was precluded from doing so; the law required the city of Dickinson to assume responsibility for the facility.

Enter Quentin N. Burdick, North Dakota's senior senator and a member of the Appropriations Subcommittee that oversees such matters as the Dickinson Dam. Siding with his constituents, Burdick inserted language in the 1984 public works appropriations bill blaming the Bureau of Reclamation for the dam troubles and directing the agency to "absorb all costs relating to the operation" of the gate and to relieve Dickinson "of all liability for property damage and personal injury which may result" from its operation.

In other words Sen. Burdick wanted the federal government to relieve the city of its obligations under the 1976 contract. Unfortunately government lawyers contend that even if the Bureau of Reclamation wanted to conform to the senator's directive, it cannot. Under terms of the authorizing statute and repayment contract, they say, the government has no legal method of relieving the city from these costs, unless the law is changed.

Long-Distance Congressional Assistance

Out in the South Pacific the U.S. trust territory of American Samoa has experienced some problems in keeping its books straight. As revealed in a FY 1983 inspector general report for the Department of Interior, the territory's government, which is supported by federal taxes, has spent beyond budget ceilings and current revenues, while shifting capital improvement funds and special grant funds over to finance its growing debt.

The problems are constantly being papered over with reams of fresh American tax dollars far in excess of what is requested by the Department of Interior. The supplemental appropriations bill of 1983 provided, at the behest of Sen. McClure, chairman of the Energy and Natural Resources Committee, $12 million for the U.S. trust territories in excess of what the administration requested. Of that amount, $7.1 million was earmarked "to be used by American Samoa to make up its projected revenue shortfall and to resolve certain financial difficulties."

Language also was included in the appropriations bill scolding American Samoa for five different areas of deficiencies, including one in which the committee recommended "civil or criminal penalties for all officials certifying illegal expenditures." At the same time, though, the committee warned the Department of Interior that it "will not tolerate any action which in any way disrupts the social or political situation as it currently exists in American Samoa." Which is to say the Department of Interior is directed not to take retributive action against American Samoa for its financial irregularities and mismanagement.

Sen. McClure has historically engineered funding for territorial programs beyond the administration's budget. The administration's FY 1983 budget request, for example, asked for $133.6 million, but Congress appropriated $169.7 million, in most cases for construction grants for which no funding had been requested that year. Moreover an extra $1.5 million was added into appropriations for Virgin Islands construction, even though the Department of Interior had never received a budget request from the Virgin Islands for FY 1983.

The Nation's "Premier Train"

Every Sunday, Wednesday, and Friday at 9:05 p.m., a sleek, silver-and-chrome train glides slowly out of Washington's Union Station en route to Chicago. It arrives 21 hours later after traveling 904 miles through the hills of western Maryland, the mountains of West Virginia, and the rolling farms of Ohio and Indiana. This is The Cardinal, and, as the name implies, it is a very special train.

If Joe and Jane Mainstreet had been inclined to take a leisurely journey, they might well have enjoyed being among the 142 riders per trip the train averaged during 1982. They could have enjoyed a hearty meal in the dining car, relaxed in the lounge car, and had their choice of comfortable reclining seats in a coach or enjoyed the privacy of a bedroom sleeper. The one-way fare for Jane and Joe together would have been $152 in coach or $314 for the bedroom sleeper.

The fares from all passengers, however, covered only 60 percent of the train's operating costs in 1982. The rest, about $2.2 million, came out of taxpayer funds. Circumstances were even worse in 1980 and 1981. Revenues then covered less than half the operating costs, and federal subsidies totaled $13.4 million for the two years.

In a major consolidation and cost-cutting effort, officials of Amtrak, the federally funded national railroad corporation, moved in late 1981 to terminate The Cardinal, along with a number of other money-losing long-distance passenger trains. Subsidized passenger trains elsewhere around the nation did end their runs—the International between Seattle and British Columbia; the North Star between Duluth and Chicago; the Inter-American between Houston, San Antonio, and Laredo, to name a few. But The Cardinal had a friend in Sen. Robert C. Byrd of West Virginia. He felt that his constituents deserved the service provided by the train, even though few of them apparently used it.

When the 1982 Transportation appropriations bill came before the Senate, Byrd moved to get The Cardinal moving again with language in the measure stating that "notwithstanding any other provision of law," Amtrak "shall provide through rail passenger service between Washington, D.C. and Chicago via Cincinnati."

Sen. Robert Packwood of Oregon tried to get the provision deleted, noting that the train did not meet the minimum ridership standard that Congress had decreed was required to continue a train and its subsidy. "If we keep this in the appropriations bill, we are saying that there is one train that is preferred," Packwood argued, even though "it does not meet any criteria that we set in statute." Asking his colleagues whether they wanted to designate a "premier train" for the nation, Packwood said: "There is no other train in this Nation that is designated by law to run."

Thanks to Sen. Byrd, though, The Cardinal has been enshrined in the law.

AIDing Boston University

Buried deep in the 50-page continuing appropriations resolution of October 1982 was a 36-word tribute of some sort to Boston University, although all it said was: "Notwithstanding any other provision of law or of this joint resolution, AID/afr-C-1414, Agency for International Development, shall be extended for an additional three years."

The Agency for International Development (AID) was preparing to wind up a five-year health-care project in West Africa run by Boston University at the end of 1982. But more than $2 million of the project's $8 million funding remained unspent. Two members of the House Foreign Affairs Committee, Clement J. Zablocki of Wisconsin, chairman of the full committee, and Howard Wolpe of Michigan, chairman of the subcommittee on Africa, were concerned that the project apparently was being ended without any appropriate follow-up action and without providing for the continued use of the "expertise and contacts" built up by Boston University in designing and implementing follow-up activities.

In a joint letter to AID, the two congressmen said that, "In a time of extreme scarcity of funds for development assistance, AID more than ever needs to demonstrate to Congress that it is reaping the maximum benefit from its expenditures." They urged that the unspent $2 million be utilized for "appropriate follow-on activities which make full use of Boston University's" ability to design and implement health programs in West Africa.

AID officials replied that they intended to draw on the experience gained through the Boston University project to examine health constraints in all of Africa, and that a new, broader, multilateral project was being assessed. Once that was done, they would be able to decide if Boston University should be awarded an exclusive contract on the basis of "predominant capability." The agency officials thought the law might require competitive bidding, in which case they expressed the hope that Boston University would "draw upon its experiences to present a solid" proposal to the agency.

Boston University was promised "fair consideration at the appropriate time," but AID officials cautioned that they also expected "great interest on the part of other firms and institutions, including minority establishments such as the historically black colleges."

As to the unspent $2 million, it was authorized as part of the previous project and so could not be used for a new, as yet undefined activity, the AID officials concluded. The congressional response to that was three lines in the continuing resolution that simply extended the project for three more years and furnished the authority to spend the $2 million. Obviously, without competition.

Education Grants

Many federal aid to education programs require competition for the grants. The law says so. Or does it? Consider the following four examples.

Example No. 1. The National Institute of Education in the Department of Education provides support to regional research centers through grants to colleges, universities, and other institutions. It does so through a competitive program in which the awards are supposed to be scheduled for recompetition every five years. When the competition was scheduled in 1979, Sen. Mark O. Hatfield of Oregon and Sen. Thomas F. Eagleton of Missouri, both members of the Appropriations Committee, inserted language in committee reports to limit the funding to those institutions already receiving grants. The effect was to ensure continued funding for two facilities in Oregon and one in Missouri, which were among the seventeen then on the list.

In 1982 Department of Education officials sought and obtained from the congressional authorizing committees approval to hold an open competition for these awards when they were due to come up again in 1984. In 1983, however, Sen. Hatfield, then chairman of the Senate Appropriations Committee, directed the institute to delay preparations for the competition, effectively killing it for 1984.

Example No. 2. Sen. Harrison Schmitt of New Mexico, a state with strong hispanic and native American communities, earmarked $650,000 in rehabilitation services and handicapped research funds for the Navajo Tribal Council in 1981. The program normally was open to competition, but the earmarking precluded other tribes from competing for the funds. The award, inserted in the 1981 budget reconciliation bill, was neither proposed nor supported by the Department of Education. It represented nearly a fourth of the $2.8 million appropriated for that activity that year.

At the insistence of Schmitt and Sen. Robert T. Stafford of Vermont, Congress inserted legislative language in a 1982 supplemental appropriation that singled out colleges with strong hispanic and native American enrollments for assistance. The effect was to direct $5.3 million, out of $10 million added to the program, to institutions almost exclusively in New Mexico and Vermont.

The program in question contained large set-asides for what are known as the historically black colleges. Schmitt's action resulted in more funds for schools in New Mexico with over 45 percent hispanic enrollment and/or native American populations that were not otherwise targeted, without reducing funds for the historically black institutions.

Example No. 3. Sen. William Proxmire of Wisconsin succeeded in directing $1.5 million in research funds to the Institute for Research on Poverty at Madison, Wis., in the face of efforts by HHS to open the funding to a competitive process. Department officials said they had been providing core support to the institute for 14 years and that it was time to broaden the horizon. But Sen. Proxmire demanded and got his share of the education pork.

Example No. 4. For many years the federal government had subsidized construction and renovation of facilities at institutions of higher learning through competitive awards. The last executive branch request for funding under this program was in 1972.

In 1981 Rep. Silvio O. Conte, with the help of House Speaker Thomas P. O'Neill, Jr., both of Massachusetts, obtained a $25 million appropriation for Georgetown University and their alma mater, Boston College. Two years later Boston College benefited again when O'Neill and another alumnus, Sen. Warren Rudman of New Hampshire, came up with $22.5 million for Boston College and the University of New Hampshire. Part of a 1983 supplemental appropriation, the $22.5 million was split: $15 million for an advanced technology and development center at the University of New Hampshire and $7.5 million for a library at Boston College.

Federal officials opposed the awards, saying they violated the program's competitive intent. In response Congress added language to the conference report on the bill specifically exempting the awards from competitive requirements in the law. Further the secretary of education was directed to waive portions of the law regarding interstate distribution of the funds, and he was prohibited from requiring the two institutions to make matching contributions, as required by law, or to hold the federal share of the project to 50 percent of the total cost. Federal officials also were directed in the same conference report to waive another section of the law requiring that grants under this program be made with the advice of a panel of experts; the report said that "no such panel currently exists and its establishment would unduly delay the disbursement of funds."

Moving Household Goods

Responding to appeals from household goods movers in Hawaii and his own state of Alaska, Sen. Ted Stevens has kept legislation in effect since FY 1978 exempting those states from the competitive rate structure governing Department of Defense (DOD) property shipments.

Stevens claimed that applying free-market principles to the movement of military household goods to his state would "adversely" affect the state's economy. To assess this claim, DOD hired a management consultant firm in 1978 to study the impact. The firm's conclusion was that "there is no reason to believe that the Competitive Rate Program would cause wide-spread economic adversity in either Alaska or Hawaii." Furthermore, 71 percent of all shipments to Alaska were found to have suffered loss or damage, compared to a 30 percent "normal" rate for DOD shipments worldwide.

Unmoved by these and other DOD findings, Stevens has continued to legislatively protect the monopoly he created. When translated into costs to the American taxpayers, this issue transcends the usual parochial concerns. During FY 1982 Alaska and Hawaii movers handled 41,000 shipments of household goods for military families at a cost of $73.8 million, of which at least $18.2 million was a hidden taxpayer subsidy above the competitive rate structure. In the five fiscal years since the Stevens amendment took effect, taxpayers have been forced to pay out $77.7 million more than they would have in a free market.

Early in 1984, Sen. Stevens flew into a rage when air force officials in Alaska sought to save $200,000 annually by purchasing milk for military bases in that state from out-of-state dairies, where prices were lower. As chairman of the Senate appropriations subcommittee on defense, Stevens promptly canceled hearings on the air force budget and served notice that not one dime would be considered for the nation's air defense until the milk "problem" was resolved. With its entire budget held hostage, the air force was forced to drop plans to stimulate competition for the milk contracts, leaving the business solely in the hands of Sen. Stevens' constituents.

70

Report . . . Report . . . Report . . . Report: Congress and the Oversight Function

> **Dingellgram** (deen'-guhl-gram) *n:* a written demand, from a member of Congress to an executive branch official, for voluminous information on programs and policies, of such detail and complexity, and with a response time so short, as to require the recipient to devote total time and attention to it, completely disregarding all other responsibilities. *vb:* to receive such a missive ("he was Dingellgrammed").

The above definition appears in no standard, or even offbeat, dictionary, yet most high-ranking bureaucrats in Washington, particularly those associated with the Department of Energy or related agencies, immediately recognize the term and its implications. It is named for Rep. John D. Dingell of Michigan, chairman of the House Energy and Commerce Committee and of its Oversight and Investigations Subcommittee, who has become known for demanding enormous amounts of information on internal agency matters, to be delivered immediately.

For example the acting head of the Department of Energy's Economic Regulatory Administration once received a four-page, single-spaced letter from Dingell that contained 51 requests or instructions for information. One request was for the status of 115 field investigations then under way by the agency. This administrator had eight working days to provide the information requested. Another Dingellgram brought forth so much paperwork a truck was required to haul the material up to the Rayburn building.

High-ranking bureaucrats, particularly presidential appointees, quickly get used to the fact that, regardless of party affiliation, much of their time in Washington is going to be spent responding to demands from Congress for information, to be supplied through written reports and/or through personal appearances at congressional hearings. Even among these hardened veterans of the political battlefields, however, one is considered to have truly arrived only after having received a Dingellgram or its equivalent.

The irony is that while the executive branch has been struggling to reduce the paperwork burden on the public, Congress has spectacularly increased the paper burden it imposes on the executive branch. Almost every piece of legislation enacted carries with it new requirements for federal managers to report to Congress on the status of a program, a research project, or some other executive branch activity, in addition to the program and budgetary information that each agency must compile and present to Congress at least once a year as part of the appropriations process.

This is on top of the innumerable demands for ad hoc reports contained in letters from committee or subcommittee chairmen seeking information on executive branch programs and plans. While most such reports are fairly brief, even they require time to prepare a response, enough of the Dingellgram variety of requests are made to cause concern among agency managers.

There is no question that Congress is entitled to information from agencies on federal programs so as to properly discharge its constitutional responsibilities. Unfortunately many of the reports Congress requires are very costly to produce, no longer relevant (if they ever were), and often not even read or used by their intended audience. Worse, despite small bows in the direction of reducing this reporting burden, Congress has given little indication that it is seriously concerned; in fact the number of reports it requires continues to increase.

According to a report by the General Accounting Office (GAO) in November 1981, statutory reports (as opposed to the ad hoc or Dingellgram type) required just by the House increased from 197 in 1930 to 1,566 in 1980, a growth of 695 percent. The growth began in the 1960s, going from 470 the year John F. Kennedy was elected president to 759 in 1970. The number has more than doubled since then, however, going to 1,566 in 1980. Coincidentally that is the same period in which Congress greatly expanded the number of subcommittees and the staff to go with them.

When the demands of the Senate are included, the 1980 figure rises to a total of 2,680 reporting requirements statutorily imposed on the federal government. This produces a total of 4,000 reports annually, because one requirement can call for more than one report. The estimated cost in 1980 to the executive branch agencies involved came to more than $80 million, according to the GAO.

In April 1980, Sen. William V. Roth, Jr. of Delaware, who later became chairman of the Senate Governmental Affairs Committee, asked GAO for a breakdown on just recurring reports. GAO responded that, based on its information, there were 1,181 reports due yearly, 142 due twice yearly; 149 due quarterly, 456 due as required, and 111 due at no special time, for a total of 2,039 recurring reports. Cost information was sketchy, but GAO was able to compile a partial cost list of $20 million. That same year, OMB submitted a proposal to Rep. Jack Brooks of Texas, chairman of the House Government Operations Committee, to eliminate or condense approximately 200 reports required by Congress. Fewer than 80 of the reports on the list were eventually deleted, for an estimated saving of $7.5 million.

Congressional reporting requirements continued to grow, however, prompting a Treasury Department official to complain to OMB that the number of reports demanded of the department had risen from 75 in 1980 to 106 in 1981, a one-year jump of 41 percent.

OMB tried again in 1982, coming back to chairman Brooks with another list of approximately 200 candidates for deletion. This time, before introducing the necessary legislation, Brooks sought the reactions of his fellow committee and subcommittee chairmen. He accepted any request to continue a report, even if no reason was given for rejecting OMB's proposal.

At a hearing on the measure in July 1982, Rep. Frank Horton of New York, the committee's ranking minority member, noted that Congress at that time generated new, recurring reports at the rate of "several hundred per Congress." Horton recalled that in 1980 a GAO witness testified that more than 2,300 congressionally mandated reporting requirements existed at that time, adding that, while 80 had been eliminated, "Congress has probably added at least that many if not more, since." He was right.

In 1982 Congress passed legislation eliminating another 80 reporting requirements, which one OMB official said came to a stack of paper in his office approximately 20 feet high. In 1983, though, GAO officials estimated that, like rabbits, the number of reporting requirements had grown to 3,500, generating a total of 4,300 reports at an estimated cost of over $86 million.

One federal manager estimated that reporting requirements for the Department of Agriculture alone jumped 68 percent from 1980 to 1983. He estimated it took some 80,982 hours of work to prepare 58 reports, for an average of 1,396 hours per report, or the equivalent of nearly 35 employees working a full year on nothing but those reports. Cost data could not be calculated for every report, but the manager was able to define costs for 53 of them, and he concluded that they came to a total of $3.2 million. That was an average of $59,526 per report, or roughly the annual salary of a deputy assistant secretary. This official also expressed concern that too many of the reports were a waste of time and effort, saying they covered too limited an area to be useful, and that too many of them were required too frequently and in too much detail. In some cases, he added, reports were required on programs no longer active or called for confidential information that, if made public, could lead to lawsuits against the agency.

In 1978, for example, Congress directed the Department of Interior to submit an annual report on natural gas wells on the Outer Continental Shelf that were not producing (shut-in) or burning off (flaring). GAO had to review and comment on the report. The aim was to determine whether well operators were deliberately holding back production in anticipation of higher prices in the future. Congress wanted to know if operators were capping wells for economic reasons or flaring gas that could be commercially used.

Interior and GAO both had said this report is unnecessary because:

- It does not do the job; Interior officials said it contains information that should be analyzed only for trends or quirks, not for determining if gas is being deliberately withheld or flared because there are other and better ways to get this information from well operators.
- Legislation and recent administration initiatives on price decontrol remove the need for concern over deliberate holding back on production of oil and gas.
- The report costs too much to produce, running to $280,000 in 1980, and both Interior and GAO officials said Congress has never paid any attention to it.

In fact GAO has produced three studies that recommend eliminating this report, but to no avail. Two efforts to get Congress to drop the report failed to gain any action.

Another report, on "Utilization of all Fee and Contract Programs," prepared by the Veterans Administration, required 186,548 staff hours and cost $1,115,000 to produce. Two Treasury Department reports, one surveying U.S. investments abroad and the other on foreign investments in the United States, cost a total of $33,950,000. Agency officials described these reports too as duplicating or overlapping with others, too expensive for the effort, and offering little evidence of their usefulness.

In addition to the formal reporting requirements, Congress keeps a close watch on government managers through a steady stream of letters, phone calls, and hearings. A quick survey of congressional liaison offices in 12 departments, for instance, revealed they received 132,221 letters from Congress during FY 1983 along with 351,823

REPORTING REQUIREMENTS BY AGENCY

The agencies responding to the largest number of reporting requirements follow:

Agency	Number of Requirements
Department of Defense	174
Department of Health, Education and Welfare*	144
Department of Interior	126
Department of State	83
Department of Agriculture	75
Department of Commerce	75
Department of Energy	75
Department of Transportation	57
General Accounting Office	57
Department of Justice	56
Department of Labor	52
Veterans Administration	51
Department of the Treasury	50

The committees which levy the largest number of reporting requirements are as follows:

Committee	Number of Requirements
Senate Committee on Governmental Affairs	386
House Committee on Government Operations	303
Joint Committee on Printing	293
House Committee on Appropriations	252
Senate Committee on Labor and Human Resources	199
Senate Committee on Appropriations	193
Senate Committee on Energy and Natural Resources	169
Senate Committee on Armed Services	164
House Committee on Armed Services	164
Senate Committee on Commerce, Science and Transportation	159
House Committee on Interstate and Foreign Commerce	151

*Includes Department of Education

75

telephone calls. Even this survey was very likely no more than a sampling, for many agencies said they did not keep count of phone calls, and the tally of letters was made only at the department level. And even that tally tells very little. One Agriculture Department agency, for example, spent $7,000 worth of staff time to prepare one report on timber information sought by one congressman.

That same year Agriculture officials spent an estimated 2,500 hours testifying at 250 hearings before various congressional committees. That works out to a minimum of one hearing a day, not counting preparation time. In addition a request by two subcommittee chairmen for information relating to wilderness legislation required the efforts of at least 50 Department of Agriculture staff persons around the nation, at an estimated cost of more than $300,000.

Federal Building Repair: "Delays, Delays, and More Delays"

At 14th and D streets, SW, in Washington, D.C., stands a five-story, L-shaped structure known as the Liberty Loan Building. Erected in 1918 it still retains its original manual elevators, leaky steam-heat radiators, and combustible ceiling tiles. Offices housing 560 employees of the Treasury Department and the General Services Administration (GSA) utilize the 98,845 square feet of space. It is a building that is almost literally flaking apart onto their shoulders.

In 1979 the House Public Works Committee approved a $3.5 million repair and alteration prospectus for the building submitted by GSA, the caretaker agency for federal buildings. This amount would have renovated the entire structure, replacing drafty wood-frame windows, adding a fire-prevention sprinkler system, and revamping the heating and cooling system to bring the building up to modern energy efficiency standards. When the proposal reached the Senate, no action was taken.

Three years later, for the 1983 budget, GSA resubmitted the prospectus—or project proposal—once again, in that conditions at the Liberty Loan Building had deteriorated markedly. This time the repair bill came to $7.2 million, the costs having more than doubled since the previous submission. Once again the Senate sat on it, another instance of Congress being paralyzed by indecision.

Numerous acts of legislation require that the executive branch furnish advance notice to congressional committees of intended actions, and then postpone these actions for a specified time to afford Congress an opportunity to alter or reject the requests. Since 1972 Congress has required GSA to submit a prospectus for any planned construction, repair, property alteration, or leasing of space if the value is $500,000 or more. These individual appropriations must be approved by both the House and Senate public works committees.

On March 12, 1979, four members of the Senate Committee on Environment and Public Works wrote a letter to GSA Administrator Joel W. Solomon to express concern about "reports of irregularities" within GSA. These abuses allegedly involved contractors being paid by GSA for work they never performed. The four senators—committee chairman Jennings Randolph of West Virginia, Daniel P. Moynihan of New York, Robert T. Stafford of Vermont, and John H. Chafee of Rhode Island—informed Solomon of their intention to enact legislation reforming the nation's public buildings policy. They also issued a warning to Solomon:

> [Until] the Congress has time to develop such a policy and . . . until such time as the Committee can act on this legislation, we have placed a moratorium on all non-emergency prospectus approvals by this Committee. It is our expectation that this process will be undertaken soon and completed during the 1st session of the 96th Congress.

Over four years have passed since these four senators instituted their moratorium. The legislation they promised would establish a new public buildings policy has not materialized into law. The paralysis revolves around a seemingly minor difference of opinion between the House and Senate. The House wants all GSA prospectuses submitted individually for review; the Senate insists on a lump sum submission for each fiscal year.

While Congress thrashes about, unable to resolve this policy dispute, the taxpayers are getting stuck for the bill. The Senate has effectively held the principal repair and alteration program of the government hostage since 1979. The original expense of necessary renovation projects has escalated sharply, as inflation, rising construction costs, and further deterioration in the buildings have taken their toll.

By October 1983 the House had approved, but the Senate Public Works Committee had failed to act on, 27 major repair and alteration projects with a combined price tag of $139.8 million (based on initial estimates). Most of the projects have been in limbo since 1978 or 1979, and, like the Liberty Loan Building, they have increased up to twofold in costs. That puts the current price tag for the taxpayers at $260 million or more.

Seven of these projects can be singled out from the GSA list as exemplifying the dimensions of the problem.

1. *Project:* Proposed alteration of post office and courthouse at New Haven, Conn.
   Date Submitted/Authorization Requested: January 3, 1979/about $4.7 million
   Date Resubmitted/Authorization Requested: June 12, 1980/about $6.8 million
   Result: Delay of 18 months at additional cost of $2.1 million
2. *Project:* Proposed alteration of post office, federal building, and courthouse at Detroit, Mich.
   Date Submitted/Authorization Requested: June 19, 1978/about $3.6 million
   Date Resubmitted/Authorization Requested: May 19, 1981/about $7.8 million
   Result: Delay of 3 years at additional cost of $4.2 million
3. *Project:* Proposed alteration of federal building at San Diego, Calif.
   Date Submitted/Authorization Requested: July 25, 1978/about $1.5 million
   Date Resubmitted/Authorization Requested: May 19, 1981/about $3 million
   Result: Delay of 3 years at additional cost of $1.5 million
4. *Project:* Proposed alteration of federal building at St. Louis, Mo.
   Date Submitted/Authorization Requested: February 23, 1979/about $4.2 million
   Date Resubmitted/Authorization Requested: May 19, 1981/about $6.1 million
   Result: Delay of 2 years at additional cost of $1.9 million
5. *Project:* Proposed alteration of federal building and courthouse at Las Vegas, Nev.
   Date Submitted/Authorization Requested: February 2, 1982/about $876,000
   Date Resubmitted/Authorization Requested: May 19, 1983/about $1.1 million
   Result: Delay of 15 months at additional cost of $203,000
6. *Project:* Proposed alteration of post office and courthouse at Scranton, Pa.
   Date Submitted/Authorization Requested: February 2, 1982/about $1.7 million
   Date Resubmitted/Authorization Requested: May 19, 1983/about $2.3 million
   Result: Delay of 15 months at additional cost of $600,000
7. *Project:* Proposed alteration of J.F. Kennedy Federal Building at Boston, Mass.
   Date Submitted/Authorization Requested: February 2, 1982/about $2.5 million
   Date Resubmitted/Authorization Requested: May 19, 1983/about $3 million
   Result: Delay of 15 months at additional cost of $500,000

Examples of Unnecessary Spending

Air Traffic Control

When the air traffic controllers went out on strike during the summer of 1981, there was some concern in Congress about the administration's ability to train enough new controllers to replace those who had left their jobs.

The Federal Aviation Administration (FAA), which has long operated its own training facility near Oklahoma City, Okla., was satisfied it could fill the needs, but Sen. Mark Andrews of North Dakota was not comforted. As chairman of the Senate's Transportation Appropriations Subcommittee, which had charge of the FAA's budget, he felt a special responsibility to ensure that enough new air controllers could be trained to fill the ranks. So language was inserted in the Transportation Department's 1982 money bill setting aside $4 million for construction at the University of North Dakota of an air traffic control center, even though FAA and Department of Transportation managers felt it could not be completed in time to be of any use in the aftermath of the strike. Even so the facility was built in Sen. Andrews's home state.

The controllers' strike served to heighten public awareness of the need for trained and competent personnel in the fields of air traffic management and safety. As aviation technology has grown more sophisticated and complex, the educational requirements for ground control and management jobs have grown more demanding. The result is a new field of education—airway science. Working with the FAA to develop a curriculum were 13 universities. Five of them, including the University of North Dakota, were accredited for the program in the spring of 1983. Just about that time the 1983 supplemental appropriation for the Department of Transportation was working its way through the Senate. The appropriations subcommittee report took notice of the "increasing and critical global importance of airway science," saying that the United States "must take a positive and energetic role in the aviation and computer technology field."

The FAA commitment must be "fulfilled and assured," the report added, so that institutions of higher learning "will have the capacity necessary to meet airway science curriculum needs," especially those which have "demonstrated an interest in and commitment to" the FAA's program.

The result was a $5 million demonstration grant for two institutions "which have shown their commitment to the improvement of airway science." The committee report instructed that one recipient be a minority institution and that the other be one "with an established program which could benefit from enhancement and acceleration."

It appears there may have been some uncertainty among FAA officials as to which institution Sen. Andrews had in mind, because a House-Senate conference report, adopted on July 20, 1983, spelled it out this way: "The conferees intend that of the funds provided at least $2,750,000 be made available to the University of North Dakota to enhance the expansion of the Airway Science Program, the other recipient has not yet been selected." The "other recipient" had still not been selected by early 1984.

Economic Research Study

Sometimes an executive branch agency is forced to fund a research project even after it demonstrates to Congress that the project would have more relevance to the mission of a different agency, or that the project will produce little of value to the taxpayers or the government.

Such was the case in the spring of 1983, when officials of the Department of Health and Human Services (HHS) sought to terminate funding for a six-year economic research project at Boston College's Social Welfare Research Institute. Known as the Multi-Regional Policy Impact Simulation Model (MRPIS), the project sought to develop a computer model that would provide detailed estimates of the economic impact of changes in government policy on various groups of people. The project had first been funded in 1980; as of 1983 HHS had spent $667,000 supporting it.

However, HHS officials had questions about the scope and feasibility of the project when applications of the model were presented in three research papers submitted to HHS in 1982. An outside consultant retained to review the papers and the project concluded that the original research plan was overly ambitious and that MRPIS would not provide results that would be helpful to the focus of HHS policy makers.

The consultant noted that MRPIS might indicate some general and regional effects of governmentwide policies and suggested that Congress or a different agency more immediately concerned with macroeconomic policy might be interested in funding the project. HHS officials agreed to explore this avenue. However, when Alice Rivlin, then director of the Congressional Budget Office, was approached in a May 1982 letter, she declined to participate. HHS officials then sought to interest other agencies, such as the Departments of Defense, Energy, Labor, and Commerce, to form a consortium to fund the project. When none expressed interest in participating, HHS officials decided not to request additional funding in 1983.

This decision soon came to the attention of the staff of Sen. Warren Rudman of New Hampshire. Rudman, a graduate of Boston College, was a member of the Senate appropriations subcommittee that funds HHS. HHS officials subsequently were called to a meeting with the senator's staff and were told to prepare to re-fund the project. That summer, in its report accompanying the FY 1983 supplemental appropriations bill, the subcommittee ordered HHS to "continue funding for this research effort at an amount necessary to keep the project on schedule, but no less than $400,000."

Falling on deaf ears in Congress was the argument by one HHS official that "if every institution that wants a grant can go to the Congress directly to obtain it, a planned, rational program of research will be impossible to organize and maintain."

Methane Gas Study

In February 1981 the Department of Energy (DOE) reviewed a proposal submitted by Yankee Refineries, Inc., of Keene, N.H., to conduct a research project for processing methane gas (a by-product of oil drilling) from offshore well operations into methanol, which can be used as a motor fuel. The idea was to use this barge-mounted operation to demonstrate the technical and engineering feasibility, as well as the commercial potential, of such an offshore undertaking. The DOE official who reviewed the proposal was highly enthusiastic, but lamented in a memorandum to a colleague that he had no funds to support it, or even to consider cost sharing.

That year, Keene was represented in the 97th Congress by freshman congressman Judd Gregg. In November and December of 1982, the 97th Congress held its famous lame-duck session. The major legislative issue on the agenda was the Surface Transportation Assistance Act of 1982, also known as the gas tax act. While the principal aspects of this $22 billion tax bill were capturing the headlines, Section 152, inserted by Rep. Gregg, was puzzling DOE officials and other observers. Section 152 required the Department of Transportation (DOT) to conduct a study of the potential for recovering methane gas released during offshore oil drilling and for converting it to methanol by using a floating plant at the drilling site. The study requirements obviously had much in common with the proposal Yankee Refineries had submitted to DOE.

The publication *Alcohol Week* indicated that DOT officials were uncertain how to handle the directive. It stated that a member of Rep. Gregg's staff was unable to say why the congressman had introduced the directive, but it did note that former congressman James C. Cleveland, Gregg's immediate predecessor in the House before retiring in 1980 after serving for 18 years, was now representing Yankee Refineries.

With no congressional language mandating a research grant, DOT officials were reluctant to spend money unnecessarily on a study. They concluded that a survey and analysis of available literature on the subject would suffice. The Senate Appropriations Committee apparently agreed, noting in its May 1983 report on a supplemental funding bill that "This topic has been studied extensively by public and private organizations, and an adequate body of literature is available for the private sector to use in judging the technical and economic feasibility of this concept." The committee went on to state that it "recommends that the Department utilize in-house personnel to accomplish the task of assembling and analyzing this literature."

The Senate was responding to action by the House Appropriations Committee, which apparently was unhappy at the way the study was being approached. Rep. Gregg certainly was too. While his amendment to the gas tax bill had made no mention of Yankee Refineries, or its earlier proposal to DOE, Gregg was not so reticent in describing what he had intended. In a February 1, 1983, letter to Rep. James J. Howard of New Jersey, chairman of the House Public Works and Transportation Committee, Gregg defined the basis of the study, pointedly noting that it "shall be completed one year from enactment under budget authority not to exceed $2,500,000."

To make sure the point got across, Rep. Gregg went on to quote liberally from the enthusiastic response of that DOE official to the Yankee Refineries proposal two years earlier, and then closed with: "I would also be extremely appreciative of any effort on your behalf to contact the Department of Transportation and indicate support for the amendment's proposal as outlined above."

Six weeks later, DOT Secretary Elizabeth H. Dole received a letter signed by 12 members of the House. They included Speaker Tip O'Neill; James Howard and the ranking minority member of his committee, Gene Snyder of Kentucky; and Glenn M. Anderson of California, chairman of the Surface Transportation Subcommittee, and his ranking minority member, E. E. ("Bud") Shuster of Pennsylvania.

The letter began: "The undersigned have a shared responsibility for and a continuing interest in the comprehensive study called for by Section 152 of the Surface Transportation Assistance Act of 1982." Expressing concern that "there is some uncertainty" at DOT as to congressional intent regarding the study, the congressmen went on to describe exactly what was expected, saying that "Only

82

a study substantially as endorsed by the Department of Energy, see attachment . . . will meet our intent for Section 152." The attachment mentioned was the enthusiastic description of the Yankee Refineries proposal to DOE.

When the 1983 supplemental appropriations bill emerged from conference several weeks later, in July 1983, it contained the following paragraph:

> The limitation on general operating expenses of the Federal Highway Administration is increased by $1,750,000 for necessary expenses to carry out the provisions of section 152 of the Surface Transportation Assistance Act of 1982 for a methane conversion study. . . .

This time Congress made sure that federal officials would not again fail to understand its intent. Rep. Joseph D. Early of Massachusetts, a member of the House Appropriations Committee, took to the House floor when the measure was up for final approval on July 29 to engage in a "brief colloquy" with William Lehman of Florida, chairman of the Transportation Appropriations Subcommittee.

After commending his colleague for adding the $1.75 million for the methane study, Early asked whether his understanding was "correct" that the funds were for a study "performed by a contractor team experienced both in low pressure, single stream methanol production from natural gas and in waterborne transportation of gas-derived energy products?" Replied Lehman, "The gentleman is correct. The House report on the supplemental appropriations bill contains such guidance to the Department of Transportation."

Right-Of-Way Costs

The Interior Department's Bureau of Land Management recovers right-of-way costs incurred by companies or individuals that build roads, pipelines, and other systems across public lands. Where costs are estimated at less than $5,000 for application processing and assessed fees, costs are based on a per-acre or per-mile estimated. For more extensive right-of-way claims, estimated in excess of $5,000, costs are recovered by Interior on a monthly billing rate connected to "actual cost" projections.

Interior sought legislation requiring applicants for right-of-way access—which are for the most part large oil and gas companies, such as Exxon—to pay access costs, starting in 1984, so that taxpayer subsidies would be unnecessary. However Sen. James A. McClure of Idaho deleted language in the FY 1984 budget bill for Interior that would have established such cost recovery. In effect the senator not only took away Interior's ability to collect about $3.5 million a year but also added $3 million in budget authority to continue federal participation, making the taxpayers poorer by $6.5 million a year.

Drug Enforcement Administration

From his position on the Senate Judiciary Committee, Sen. Dennis DeConcini of Arizona has launched his own coordinated attack on the nation's drug problem, directing the Treasury and Justice departments in their efforts to staunch the flow of illicit substances.

DeConcini inserted language into the committee report for the Treasury Department's 1984 appropriations bill telling the U.S. Customs Service to establish a radar command and control center in his hometown of Tucson, Ariz., even though Treasury wanted the control center elsewhere. DeConcini answered potential criticism this way:

> "[T]he Committee sees no inconsistency or duplication involved in establishing a . . . [command and control center in] . . . Tucson and the goals of the national narcotics drug interdiction program in the area of radar surveillance and communication."

The committee report for the 1983 supplemental appropriations bill for the Department of Justice reflected Sen. DeConcini's conviction that the Drug Enforcement Administration (DEA) should give out more bribe money, saying that "our concern [is] that insufficient funds are available to DEA offices in land-border States for information and evidence. The Committee directed that DEA allocate a minimum of $10,000 to each land-border State for such purposes. . . ."

Customs Officials at Laredo

Congress has a number of ways of informing government agencies exactly how they want taxpayer dollars spent, in addition to writing instructions into laws and committee reports. When offering an amendment on the floor to an appropriations bill, for which specific instructions would be out of order, a member can simply stand up and say how he wants it spent. That statement then becomes legislative history, which the agencies generally follow closely and to which even the courts look for guidance.

84

That is just what Rep. Abraham Kazen, Jr. of Texas did in 1982. His district includes Laredo, which is a major tourist crossing point on the U.S.–Mexican border. Kazen wanted the U.S. Customs Service to beef up the staff there because lines of waiting cars would sometimes extend back for two miles from the border post.

So, when he proposed to add $5 million to a spending bill in November 1982, Rep. Kazen wanted to make sure it was spent for more customs officials at Laredo. He did that by engaging in a colloquy with another member.

After being recognized by the chairman and announcing that he was offering an amendment to add $5 million to the bill, Kazen described the problem in Laredo. At this point Rep. Edward R. Roybal of California, whose district also borders Mexico, rose and addressed Kazen. Their conversation went like this:

> *Mr. Roybal:* "Do I understand the gentleman correctly when he states that his amendment provides for $5 million additional?"
>
> *Mr. Kazen:* "That is correct."
>
> *Mr. Roybal:* "And that money is to . . . pay for personnel along the border?"
>
> *Mr. Kazen:* "That is correct. . . . I cannot, as you well know, specify in the bill that particular provision. But, in order to make legislative history, this colloquy between you and me should serve as directive to the Customs agency that this is what the Congress intends these $5 million to be used for."

The amendment was adopted, as was the bill.

Mining Scholarship

There is not a great demand for mining engineers these days. The Society of Mining Engineers decided against setting aside special job-interviewing facilities at its March 1982 meeting after a survey showed that only one of 9,392 respondents had a job open and was interested in seeing applicants. According to information provided to Sen. James A. McClure of Idaho, chairman of the Senate Interior Appropriations Subcommittee, at a hearing in March 1983, there were only 1,317 mining engineer degrees awarded in the United States in 1982.

Then why is the federal government spending $9.3 million annually on a program for mining research and training?

One reason may be that $4.6 million of that money is intended for scholarships and fellowships at 31 mining schools around the country. One of them is the University of Idaho, which had received $910,000 over the previous three years and was in line to receive an estimated $300,000 to $400,000 for FY 1984.

Federal officials have been trying to drop this program for several years, but the money keeps popping back up in appropriations bills. Sen. McClure told Department of Interior officials at the hearing in March 1983 he was "happy to note" that they were no longer proposing to zero-fund the program on grounds the institutions involved "are not 'uniquely federal'."

"This year," McClure observed, "you have proposed them for no funding because the institutions have other sources of public and private support" to help meet their programs. When he asked if any private sources had been tapped to pick up the slack should federal funding end, McClure was told that Standard Oil of Ohio had announced a $10 million program for research, with a "fair portion" of that in mineral industries.

Nevertheless McClure reinserted the federal subsidy to train mining engineers who were not needed.

The Redding Courthouse

There was no federal courthouse in the northern California town of Redding in 1983, but not for want of trying by its long-time congressman, Harold T. ("Bizz") Johnson. From his post as chairman of the House Public Works and Transportation Committee, Johnson inserted $12.8 million for a courthouse even though there was no federal judge assigned to sit in its chambers. Furthermore the other federal tenant assigned to the building, the Department of Agriculture, said it did not need the additional space the building would provide.

Before construction on the project began, Rep. Johnson was defeated for reelection in 1980. With no one to push for the planned courthouse, GSA persuaded the House Appropriations Committee to let it shift the funds to other purposes.

IV. The Agency People: How Congress Tries to Manage Executive Branch Human Resources

A standard principle of sound management is that administrators must have the authority to make employee assignments so as to obtain the most effective use of employees, and also the flexibility to change assignments to meet changing program needs or to improve the efficiency or delivery of services. Members of Congress have stated no less themselves.

Yet, in the short lifetime of this survey, the PPSSCC has found numerous personnel directives from Congress specifying numbers and types of personnel for specified programs, offices, and facilities. Congress has even directed specific wage levels in specific offices without regard to the impact nationally on wage scales.

Too often, it would appear, Congress has intervened in executive branch management of human resources with directives that have preserved the status quo of jobs for federal employees at the expense of proposals that would have reduced costs or improved efficiencies. It is almost as though Congress has added to its role that of protecting federal employees against the kinds of change and challenge that executives and employees in the private sector face all the time.

Mandating Personnel Management Decisions

The Committee has no intent to interfere in the management prerogatives of the Executive. Administrators must have the flexibility to assign resources to meet changing program needs.

—Senate Appropriations Subcommittee for Commerce, Justice and State, 1982 Report.

Imagine the head of a $26 billion operation with over 200,000 employees who must obtain the approval of his board of directors for any reorganization plan that will affect as few as three employees—and who must then wait eight months to implement the plan.

Then meet the head of the Veterans Administration (VA). Under language enacted into law in 1981, the VA administrator must submit a detailed plan to Congress for any administrative reorganization plan that will affect 10 percent or more of the permanent full-time equivalent employees at a "covered office or facility." That last term means any VA office or facility that has 25 or more permanent employees or that is a freestanding outpatient clinic. In addition the administrator must submit the plan to Congress the same day the president submits the next fiscal year's budget. Since that must be done in February, it means Congress has until October 1, when the new fiscal year starts, to micromanage that plan.

Congress defines "administrative reorganization" as "consolidation, elimination, abolition, or redistribution of functions" in the agency. For nearly a quarter century, the VA administrator had held exactly that authority, along with the authority to create new agency functions as they were needed. In short, until 1981, the VA administrator was in fact the administrator.

Why this radical "redistribution" of authority?

It is part of a broad, new, and some may say disturbing pattern that has been evolving in recent years, in which the Congress has assumed the role of protector of the permanent government structure against any change other than expansion.

Ironically the legislative vehicle used to tie up the VA this way was a bill that was requested by the administration. It was to provide an 11 percent cost-of-living increase in pensions for disabled veterans and their dependents and survivors.

The $1 billion measure also included provisions related to housing, insurance, and even headstones and marker and memorial areas for deceased veterans. At that time the VA was contemplating major reorganizational and staffing changes as part of a governmentwide effort to streamline costs and determine federal priorities and responsibilities. Reflecting Capitol Hill concerns about this effort, the bill emerged from the Senate in late July 1981 with language designed to ensure that the agency would adhere to personnel levels indicated by Congress. Nonetheless the measure passed by voice vote, almost without debate.

The House was not satisfied, however. Rep. Marvin Leath of Texas, a member of both the Armed Services and Veterans' Affairs committees, proposed language that was both broader and more restrictive with respect to the role of the VA administrator. He suggested that Congress require reorganization plans to be submitted for a 60-day review, during which time either body could vote to reject it (this was a one-house legislative veto, the kind later struck down by the U.S. Supreme Court). Leath said, "This will allow Congress to monitor the VA offices and hospitals, which are of major concern to our veterans." This provision went almost unnoticed on the House floor, as the bill was adopted by a voice vote on September 21 under a special procedure that the House reserves for measures considered minor, routine, or without controversy.

When the Veterans Compensation Amendments Act emerged from a House-Senate conference ten days later, the one-house veto provision was gone. It had been replaced by language that virtually shifted personnel management authority from the VA administrator to Congress by requiring submission of detailed plans when as few as three employees might be involved, and forcing the administrator to await congressional approval, which could take up to eight months. Sen. Alan K. Simpson of Wyoming, chairman of the Senate Armed Services Committee, explained the change to his colleagues by saying he could not accept a one-house veto "in this instance." It could "impair" attempts by administration officials to make changes they determine are "necessary to constitute an effective use of employees, programs and . . . fiscal resources."

Sen. Simpson, who had introduced the original bill on behalf of the administration five months earlier, added that a legislative veto "would not encourage open communication between the Congress, the Administration and the Veterans Administration."

Of the final provision requiring the VA administrator to obtain congressional approval for a plan that could affect as few as three employees, Simpson said the "compromise agreement contains a very equitable solution" in that it offers "ample time for Congressional comment and dialogue with the Veterans Administration." Congressional involvement in personnel was nothing new in 1981, but never before had there been such attention to detail on such a broad scale.

While the VA was perhaps the only federal agency tied up in law in quite this way, many other agencies found themselves with a myriad of congressional personnel directives. Most came in the form of language in committee reports accompanying appropriations bills, as Congress sought to use its power of the purse strings to mandate specific numbers of federal employees in specific locations in the early 1980s—the period scanned in this report.

The aim was usually to prevent an agency from reducing personnel or transferring them as part of a reorganization or consolidation effort. The numbers involved often were small, ranging down to two scientists at an agricultural research station in Florida, and one attorney in the Farmers Home Administration office in Stillwater, Okla. Occasionally, though, the numbers were on a broader scale, as when Rep. Gerry E. Studds of Massachusetts, chairman of the Coast Guard and Navigation Subcommittee, inserted language in the coast guard's 1982 authorization bill requiring the agency to maintain at least 5,484 civilian employees throughout FY 1983 and FY 1984.

Committee reports lack the full and direct force of law, such as is found in authorization language. But it has often been easier for members of Congress to put language in a report than into the law itself, especially in the appropriations process. In addition, even though government lawyers have argued that an agency need not consider committee reports to be as binding as legislation, most federal administrators have hesitated to make a habit of flouting or directly challenging any directives contained in those reports. After all, next year's regular appropriations bill is already in the works— and this year's urgent supplemental appropriation may be coming around even sooner.

In some cases it could be argued that Congress was using personnel micromanaging through the appropriations process as a way to fight policy battles with the administration. In other cases it may be more readily apparent as an effort to seek or retain control over an agency's structure, as in the VA reorganization directive. Whatever Congress' motive, even a brief survey of appropriations subcommittee reports disclosed a broad pattern of personnel micromanagement, especially among those agencies perceived as policy battlegrounds.

In the 1982 supplemental appropriations act for the Department of Energy (DOE), for example, Congress not only wrote into law specific personnel numbers for designated offices but also earmarked where some individuals would go. DOE's assistant secretary for conservation and renewables was allocated 352 employees, with 95 percent of them designated for specific offices: 154 to conservation research and development activities, 180 to state and local conservation activities. DOE's assistant secretary for fossil energy had 530 of his 754 employees designated for the Pittsburgh and Morgantown, W. Va., energy technology centers. Of the 450 employees allocated to the Economic Regulatory Administration, 160 were designated to be auditors and 40 were assigned to the Office of Fuels Conversion.

A year later the assistant secretary for fossil energy and the administrator of the Economic Regulatory Administration were allowed to reduce their personnel levels by a combined total of 109 employees. For them to accomplish this the law had to be amended to reflect the new numbers. The new legislation read this way:

> Notwithstanding section 303(3) of Public Law 97-257, funds provided for Economic Regulatory Administration by this or any other Act shall be used (1) to maintain not less than three hundred and eighty full-time permanent Federal employees, of which not less than forty employees shall be assigned to the Office of Fuels Conversion, for the fiscal year ending September 30, 1983; and (2) to maintain not less than three hundred and five full-time equivalent Federal employees, of which not less than twenty-seven employees shall be assigned to the Office of Fuels Conversion for the fiscal year ending September 30, 1984: Provided further, that notwithstanding any other provision of law, the minimum employment level established in Public Law 97-257 for the Office of the Assistant Secretary for Fossil Energy is reduced to 715 with no further amendment to the suballocations therein.

In other words the entire legislative mechanism of the U.S. government was thrown into gear to affect 109 job slots, which constituted 5 percent of the 2,046 covered the previous year, and 0.6 percent of the 17,000 employees in the Department of Energy.

More recently the House Energy and Water Appropriations Subcommittee (formerly known as the Public Works Subcommittee) designated in its report for the 1984 appropriations bill $17.5 million for 333 employees for DOE's materials production program, of whom 277 were for the Savannah River operations office.

The Environmental Protection Agency (EPA) is another executive branch agency that has felt the fine but heavy hand of its congressional appropriations committees in recent years, although none of their directives have been written into law, as was the case with DOE.

As part of an effort to cut costs and refine operations, EPA managers proposed a budget of $540.4 million for employee salaries and expenses for FY 1984, a cut of $8.2 million, or 1.5 percent, from the FY 1983 appropriation of $548.6 million. Congress responded by refusing to accept the proposed cuts. Instead Congress increased the 1984 appropriation over the 1983 level by $26.3 million, or 4.7 percent, and increased spending above the executive branch proposal by $34.5 million, or 6.3 percent, to a total of $574.9 million. In addition Congress directed in the House-Senate conference report accompanying the 1984 spending bill the allocation of 193 EPA employees in nine specific instructions, as follows:

1. Eight positions for the EPA laboratory at Grosse Isle, Mich., located in the district of Rep. John D. Dingell.
2. Ten positions for review of advanced wastewater treatment construction grants projects at the agency's Washington, D.C., office.
3. Forty positions for the pesticide program.
4. Twenty positions for toxic chemical activities.
5. Thirty-five positions for the inspector general's office.
6. Forty positions for health risk assessments.
7. Thirty positions for air- and water-quality monitoring and enforcement.
8. Five positions for implementing strategies arising from the agency's massive study of the Chesapeake Bay.
9. Five positions for waste disposal research.

Following are some other examples of how Congress has micro-managed personnel in the executive branch.

Department of Commerce

The Senate appropriations subcommittee with jurisdiction for the budget of the National Oceanographic and Atmospheric Administration specified in its report with the FY 1982 spending bill that $4.1 million had been added to maintain staffing at the 1981 year-end level. This prevented any reductions by the administration. The same panel also served notice of its intention that the National Technology Telecommunications and Information Administration "retain at least 16 of the 19 employees proposed for separation." In that same report the senators observed that the subcommittee "has no intent to interfere in the management prerogatives of the Executive. Administrators must have the flexibility to assign resources to meet changing program needs."

Department of Justice

In 1948, when the Department of Justice established an antitrust office in Cleveland, Ohio, that city was still one of the nation's leading centers of commerce and industry. The list of major corporations with headquarters there included Standard Oil of Ohio, White Consolidated, Diamond Shamrock, American Ship Building, and Addressograph/Multigraph. By 1983 most of those corporate giants had moved out, and the Cleveland antitrust office, with a staff of 19 federal attorneys, had a considerably smaller case load. With the number of antitrust cases off nationwide, Department of Justice officials proposed transferring 55 U.S. attorneys, including the 19 in Cleveland, from the antitrust division to other offices with heavier case loads. All told, 125 attorneys would be shifted. The department proposed to reallocate $6.1 million from its General Legal Activities and Antitrust Division appropriations to pay for the moves.

The 19 Cleveland attorneys did not want to move. Ohio's senators, John Glenn and Howard M. Metzenbaum, along with the state's House delegation, also wanted to keep the Cleveland office open, and they persuaded the Senate and House appropriations committees to reject the requested shift of funds. The Department of Justice has been able to move many other attorneys anyway, but the Cleveland antitrust office with its 19 staff attorneys remains open for business.

Department of Education

To improve its rate of collections on student loans, the Department of Education went to outside contractors. They had been so successful that the department proposed to reduce its regular staff in that activity and consolidate collections in San Francisco, with savings of $5 million in FY 1983 and FY 1984.

Sen. Charles H. Percy of Illinois, however, inserted language in the 1983 supplemental appropriations bill saying that despite the achievements of outside contractors, "it is not the [Congress's] intention that the Department reduce its own collection staff." The department was told to continue to employ 382 full-time student loan collectors, and to maintain operations in the Chicago, Atlanta, and San Francisco offices. The Chicago staff numbered 116.

Department of Labor

The Department of Labor's Veterans Employment Service consists of a network of veterans' employment representatives. Although paid by the federal government, they work in the offices of state employment service administrations, looking out for veterans' interests in government jobs and training programs. Each representative is assigned a secretary who, although considered a state employee, is paid partly by federal funds.

In 1979 and again in 1982, Department of Labor managers sought to shift the secretaries off the federal payroll, saying there was serious doubt that they were needed in the federal structure. Fifty-two positions and a total of $970,000 was at stake in 1982. Both in 1979 and 1982, with Sen. Quentin M. Burdick of North Dakota and Sen. Harrison Schmitt of New Mexico taking the lead, Congress refused to allow the Department of Labor to eliminate the positions.

The new jobs training act passed in 1982 was designed to reduce the direct federal role that had characterized this area at least since the 1930s. As federal managers moved to shift resources, though, Congress often declined to go along. One result of the new approach, for example, was to be a reduced load on the Job Corps. But, when federal managers sought to cut excess staffing levels and save $4 million, Congress said no. The House appropriations subcommittee with jurisdiction over the Labor Department said in its report for the FY 1984 spending bill that "the Committee expects the existing Federal staffing levels for this program to be maintained."

Department of Agriculture

The Department of Agriculture also was subjected to some personnel fine tuning by Congress in FY 1983 and FY 1984. The department received directives to

- Place two full-time staff attorneys in Alaska at the disposal of the National Forest Service's regional forester there. In addition the general counsel, the nominal boss of the attorneys, was ordered to allocate enough funds to hire secretaries for the two.
- Replace two recently retired employees of the soil, water, air, and plant program at the Fort Pierce, Fla., agricultural research station with "other ARS employees of equal ability and to otherwise maintain USDA participation in this program consistent with past efforts."
- Allocate and fill three additional engineering positions at the Morgantown, W. Va., office of the Soil Conservation Service.
- Not transfer personnel or terminate programs of Ohio State University's Horticultural Insects Research Laboratory at Wooster, Ohio.

Defense Department

Congressional involvement in personnel goes beyond simply parceling out job slots like a card dealer. Sometimes members of Congress become involved in determining just how much a federal worker should get paid. In the process they sometimes get carried away.

Hourly wage rates for federal blue-collar employees, such as carpenters, painters, and mechanics, are determined by surveying what their counterparts are paid by private industry in the community. Thus, because of differences in the general cost of living from community to community, wage scales can differ.

Which brings us to Wichita, Kans., home of McConnell Air Force Base, the 184th Air National Guard, and Rep. Dan Glickman.

Federal blue-collar workers at the base were upset in 1981, claiming their pay envelopes were unfairly slimmer than those of counterpart workers in comparable cities such as Topeka and Oklahoma City. At the time the federal blue-collar wage in Wichita was $7.69 an hour, compared to $8.53 in Topeka and $9 in Oklahoma City.

Rep. Glickman and Sen. Nancy L. Kassebaum of Kansas rose to their defense, arguing that their constituents were victims of an error in the survey used in setting wage scales. The error needed to be set right with special legislation. In July 1981 Glickman asked his colleagues on the House Defense Appropriations Subcommittee for help in "remedying a very serious problem" at McConnell, saying it posed a "very real impact on our defense preparedness."

"Corrective action is critically needed," Glickman said, claiming that worker retention at the base had become a "major problem." Federal personnel officials said, however, that the data did not show that Wichita differed materially in that regard from other areas. Calling the Wichita situation "unique," Glickman assured his colleagues that special legislation bringing his constituents up to "par" with their federal counterparts elsewhere would not lead to a "flood of increases across the country."

That fall the secretary of defense was directed, in the 1982 continuing resolution, to "correct the wage grade rate disparity" of civilian employees at the 184th. Sen. Kassebaum and Rep. Glickman later added language to the defense appropriations bill exempting those workers from the 4.8 percent limit on pay raises that affected all other federal employees. Result: In January 1982 federal blue-collar workers at the 184th Air National Guard Tactical Fighter

Group picked up a 27.8 percent pay raise, bringing them to $10.51 an hour. Based on a 40-hour work week, they went from $307.60 a week, $33.60 behind their better-paid brethren in Topeka, to $420.40 a week, $49.28 ahead of their upstate Topeka brethren.

The fight between Congress and the executive branch over personnel mandates is not new, but the examples reviewed here barely suggest the issues involved. What is new is the expanding scope, breadth, and depth of this congressional intrusion.

As recently as 1979 there was some concern in a few sectors of Congress over intrusion into management aspects of government agencies. A Senate committee report that year, for example, agreed with a House report finding that personnel ceilings imposed by OMB on various agencies "resulted in program inefficiencies" and use of appropriated funds for purposes other than intended by Congress. But the Senate committee concluded "reluctantly" that imposing legislated personnel minimums was a poor response to the issue. The committee said it found "persuasive" the administration's arguments that provisions which "specify personnel numbers or total salary levels are legislative encroachments on the Executive power of program management."

Congress also bears a "significant responsibility" in "assuring sound management" of programs and efficient use of tax dollars, the committee said. On balance, though, it recommended deletion of provisions in the bill that spelled out specified salary costs and personnel numbers.

Consumer Product Safety Commission

By 1983 some elements in Congress were willing not only to insist upon minimum personnel levels (even if an agency said it did not need and could not use the added numbers) but also to assert that one agency in particular would make personnel and related budgetary decisions independently of the budget process of the executive branch.

Such was the case in June 1983, when the House considered a bill put forward by Rep. Henry A. Waxman of California, chairman of the subcommittee with jurisdiction over the Consumer Product Safety Commission (CPSC). Rep. Waxman's measure extended the authority of the CPSC for five years, changed some procedural practices, and raised the funding level by $13 million, or 38 percent, over its current operations, and another $10 million over the ensuing four years, for a total increase of 68 percent.

96

Even though the CPSC itself said it did not need that much additional money, the real issue in the 20-page measure was a paragraph stating:

> The Commission shall employ on a permanent basis not fewer than the full-time equivalent of 650 officers and employees. Any decision of the Commission to employ more than the full-time equivalent of 650 officers and employees shall not be subject, directly or indirectly, to review or approval by any person within the Executive Office of the President.

In other words the agency not only would be required to maintain a minimum number of employees on the payroll, whether or not they were needed, but also would be free to hire as many more as it could justify to *Congress*, not the president.

Rep. Waxman argued that as an "independent regulatory agency," the CPSC "is not part of the administration itself." Accusing the administration of trying to gut the agency, Waxman said that "one way for an independent agency to be made less independent is . . . to try to reduce its personnel levels, even if Congress authorizes and appropriates sufficient funds to employ those people."

But Rep. Richard C. Shelby of Alabama, a member of Rep. Waxman's subcommittee, strongly opposed the measure, not only because of its expense but also because of the directive on personnel. "It is intrusive and presumptuous on the part of Congress to interject itself into this entirely management function," Shelby said. "It is congressional arrogance to obstruct executive agency personnel . . . decision making," especially, he added, when the CPSC itself said it could operate effectively with 624 employees, 26 fewer than the minimum mandated in Waxman's bill.

In a rare act of defiance of one's own subcommittee chairman, Shelby offered an amendment on the House floor that eliminated the personnel directives, saying: "I do not see how we as Members of Congress can mandate functions for management of personnel around the country. . . . [T]his is clearly a job for the executive branch of Government." Shelby's amendment was adopted by a 238-177 vote, implying that 177 members of the House supported the Waxman provision. That is only 41 short of an absolute majority, and well within striking distance of the 200 or so votes that most bills need to pass (after figuring absentees).

Rep. Shelby and others focused on the personnel directives in the Waxman proposal, as well as its cost, while Rep. Waxman sought to couch the terms of the debate as a pro- or anti-consumer argument. Those who supported him, he implied, were pro-consumer, meaning that those who opposed him were therefore anti-consumer.

With item veto authority, a president could veto that one paragraph in the bill while accepting the rest. As matters now stand, a president would have to veto the entire bill and thereby risk accusations of being anti-consumer.

Contracting Out: "No (Outside) Help Wanted"

When OMB early in 1984 sought to conduct feasibility studies of contracting out certain maintenance operations of the nation's 334 federal parks and recreation areas, three members of Congress quickly introduced legislation to thwart the entire process. Despite indications that reliance on the private sector rather than federal employees might save millions of dollars annually, Sen. Robert C. Byrd of West Virginia, Sen. Max Baucus of Montana, and Sen. Dale Bumpers of Arkansas moved to have the National Park Service (NPS) exempted from any contracting-out initiatives. The senators were responding to pleas from NPS personnel that "private contractors likely would not share the devotion of longtime park employees" to the environment. This is but one more recent example of a trend Congress has set in motion to frustrate every executive branch effort to save taxpayers money by reducing the role of federal employees in menial or commercial activities.

On January 1, 1955, the Eisenhower administration first officially adopted a policy of relying on the private sector for commercial goods and services, a response to recommendations from the Hoover commission on economizing. Bureau of the Budget bulletins issued in 1955, 1957, and 1960 defined and refined the contracting-out policy.

OMB first issued Circular A-76 in 1966 to prescribe detailed procedures for implementing that policy. The circular, which was revised in 1967, 1979, and more recently in August 1983, declares:

> In the process of governing, the Government should not compete with its citizens. The competitive enterprise system, characterized by individual freedom and initiative, is the primary source of national economic strength. In recognition of this principle, it has been and continues to be the general policy of the Government to rely on commercial sources to supply the products and services the Government needs.

Compared to the private sector, federal government performance of commercial operations is overstaffed, overpaid, and top-heavy with expensive supervisors. According to a GAO investigation, "it costs GSA [General Services Administration] over 50 percent more to clean with its in-house staff than with contractors and nearly twice as much as its landlords pay to clean leased Federal offices."

The Grace commission task force report entitled Personnel Management estimated that the federal government could save at least $1 billion annually by contracting out these services, which include such jobs as those of custodian, lawnkeeper, and elevator operator. Twenty-nine years after the policy of reliance on the private sector was first promulgated, there are 400,000 to 500,000 federal employees engaged in activities that could be performed at less cost by the private sector. Within the United States and its possessions, where A-76 applies, and excluding the U.S. Postal Service, at least one out of every five executive branch civilian employees is performing a commercial function. These employees are involved in about 11,000 separate commercial activities, costing approximately $20 billion a year.

In August 1983, on issuing new instructions to the agencies, an OMB official declared that if the policy of reliance on the private sector were fully carried out, the annual savings to the U.S. taxpayers would amount to $5 billion within five years.

But the policy of contracting out has been poorly implemented at best. A 1978 report by GAO concluded: "Although it has been the Executive Branch's general policy since 1955 to rely on contractors for those commercial goods and services, agency compliance with this policy has been inconsistent and ineffective."

Why has there been such a lack of success in carrying out a policy endorsed by every administration over the past 29 years? At a time when most lawmakers profess concern about the mounting costs of government, why has the federal government failed to turn to the private sector for commercial services it provides more effectively, and thereby save taxpayers up to $5 billion a year?

Congress must share a large measure of the blame, for it has failed to enact a national policy supporting contracting out to the private sector. In a September 1978 report, GAO found that "the A-76 policy was not perceived as a national policy with full executive and legislative branch approval and support." GAO concluded that this absence of a legislated national policy contributed to the inconsistent implementation of A-76 by the executive agencies, and it recommended that Congress enact a clear policy of support for contracting out. A second GAO report in June 1981 came to similar conclusions.

Although OMB under the Carter administration had in 1978 opposed any enactment of a national policy, that position changed when it came under the Reagan administration. In August 1983, commenting upon a bill called the Freedom From Government Competition Act, that would require the government to procure goods and services from the private sector, David A. Stockman, director of OMB, stated:

> Piecemeal legislative restrictions over the past several years have made it difficult to issue a clear-cut policy. The current policy has evolved from compromise reached with various interests and our commitment to equity to all parties. Even with the current A-76 policy of fairness, there are several statutes and proposed Congressional restrictions that will limit our ability to implement this policy fully. The Administration would welcome a clear statement by the Congress upon which to base a firm and long lasting A-76 policy.

Congress had slapped a six-month moratorium on A-76 cost studies by the Defense Department in August 1982, vowing to use those six months to enact a national policy on how the federal government would acquire its goods and services. The moratorium period came and went, and Congress never acted.

This very absence of a national policy on contracting out has probably aided individual legislators in their attempts to tack onto appropriation or authorization legislation specific riders to preserve the jobs of local constituents employed by the federal government who might have been affected by contracting out. Growing opposition to contracting out from federal employee unions, beginning in earnest in about 1977, also prompted some members of Congress to launch piecemeal legislative assaults on any attempt by the agencies, no matter now minor, to contract out.

Following is the sequence of restrictions:

1. *FY 1978 Defense Authorization Act.* An amendment required DOD to follow its regulations prior to June 1976 in making cost comparisons between federal employee and contract employee work. This amendment required DOD to use a federal retirement benefit factor of 7.14 percent instead of 24.7

percent, thus patently understating federal costs and biasing results in favor of retaining job functions in-house. It explains in part why the executive branch itself began juggling the same benefit factor for political reasons. This amendment actually did not take effect because it was overtaken by an even stronger restriction.

2. *FY 1978 Defense Appropriation Act.* Reps. Richard C. White and Abraham Kazen, Jr. of Texas were instrumental in enacting a provision that placed a moratorium on DOD contracting out certain major functions during FY 1978.

3. *FY 1979 Defense Authorization Act.* An amendment continued the moratorium until DOD submitted a report to Congress on changes in DOD regulations.

4. *FY 1981 Defense Appropriation Act.* Reps. White and Kazen of Texas, along with Rep. William Nichols of Alabama, inserted permanent restrictions and requirements: DOD could not contract out to circumvent personnel ceilings; before converting any activity costing $100,000 or more, DOD must (1) notify Congress of a decision to make a cost study, (2) provide Congress with a summary of the cost comparison, (3) certify that the government estimate is based on the most efficient organization, and (4) report to Congress on the effect of a conversion on government employees, the community, and the military mission.*

5. *FY 1981 Defense Appropriation Act.* Rep. Samuel Gejdenson of Connecticut inserted a provision for a one-year moratorium on contracting out fire protection and security services. Rep. Victor Fazio of California sponsored a provision for a six-month moratorium on all new cost studies, except for food, custodial, garbage, and laundry services.

6. *Veterans Compensation, Education, and Employment Act, Amendments of 1982.* An amendment sponsored by Rep. Marvin Leath

---

*Congress has not imposed similar requirements for reporting or cost comparison studies on the civilian agencies. Unlike DOD, civilian agencies do not furnish Congress with notices or reports of each cost comparison study and contract action. Under current A-76 procedures, civilian agencies are generally required to make cost comparison studies if more than ten federal employees are affected, but need not make such studies when the agency determines there is no chance in-house performance would be economical. The Reagan administration has several times requested Congress to remove the DOD requirements as being unreasonable and costly, but Congress has refused.

of Texas effectively prevented contracting out patient care or activities incident to patient care in veterans' hospitals, three of which can be found in his district.

7. *FY 1983 Appropriations for Treasury, U.S. Postal Service, and GSA, Continuing Resolution.* Rep. Robert W. Edgar of Pennsylvania sponsored an amendment that imposed a moratorium on GSA for FY 1983 on contracting out for the services of guards, custodians, elevator operators, and messengers.

8. *FY 1984 Defense Authorization Bill.* Rep. Earl Hutto of Florida and Sen. George J. Mitchell of Maine introduced an amendment that imposed a two-year moratorium on contracting out for fire-fighting and security services and also required DOD to submit to Congress a comprehensive report on the A-76 program, including current data on prior conversions.

Many other legislative attempts to impose additional restrictions on contracting out were not adopted. This steady stream of congressional opposition explains in part the administration's lack of resolve to proceed fully with its own policy of reliance upon the private sector. Here are three examples of restrictive bills introduced but not enacted:

- Rep. Bill Nichols of Alabama proposed an amendment to the Uniformed Services Pay Act of 1982 that would have required the cost of conducting cost comparison studies to be included as a cost of contracting out. A typical cost study takes from 9 to 24 months to complete, and weighting the costs of such studies on the contractor would significantly bias the results in favor of retaining the function on an in-house basis.

- Rep. Marvin Leath of Texas introduced a bill that would have imposed a governmentwide, permanent ban on contracting out custodian, elevator operator, messenger, and guard functions.

- Rep. Marjorie S. Holt of Maryland introduced an amendment to the FY 1984 Defense Authorization Act that would have imposed a one-year moratorium on private contracting at the three service academies. This bill was prompted by Holt's misunderstanding of why U.S. Naval Academy midshipmen were performing such menial tasks as those of custodians and kitchen aides. She thought it was due to the failure of private contractors to perform. Actually it was due to federal civil servants halting work after learning that their functions would be contracted out (many functions had previously been contracted out at West Point and the air force academies with favorable results and sizable savings). The Holt amendment passed the House but died in the Senate after the mistake was discovered. Notwithstanding, the navy notified Holt it would postpone eliminating the positions of the federal civil servants who had walked off the job. This is a vivid example of how congressional influence is registered.

With such a steady flow of restrictions and proposed restrictions from Congress, it is understandable that the executive branch's commitment to A-76 policies has waivered. As GAO observed in 1978 and 1981 reports, with respect to executive branch policy, the "emphasis has shifted from almost outright reliance on the private sector to reliance with exceptions."

Individual members of Congress are quick to interfere in decisions on whether to contract out a specific function at a specific location. Their intervention always has been on the side of the opposition to contracting out.

Under A-76 procedures, affected parties have the right to appeal cost comparison decisions to the agencies making the decisions, and they usually do. Losing parties, however, still may not be happy with the agency's final decision, at which point they may bring the matter to the attention of their congressional representatives.

In attempting to favor their constituents, individual congressmen frequently find themselves intervening to represent the views of the threatened federal employees, or their unions, in opposition to contracting out. Manifestly their influence is employed for parochial reasons rather than in the national interest.

This prevalent type of congressional interference also has several objectionable effects upon executive actions. Federal managers are inhibited from taking actions to contract out, regardless of possible savings, if it means being subjected to pressures from Congress. The attitude of the federal manager often becomes why bother, since he has nothing to gain personally but trouble by contracting out.

While a proposal for contracting out is under consideration, the intervention of an influential congressman may swing the decision against contracting out, regardless of the merits. Even if the congressman is ultimately unable to block a contract, he nonetheless can delay it for months or years.

Deliberate congressional acts held up a contract to provide base operation services at Fort Gordon, Georgia. The same work formerly performed by 1,400 federal employees is now being performed by a contractor using 1,100 employees. A GAO review of this contract found that of the federal positions eliminated, 479 were military personnel who were released from performing commercial functions and reassigned to military duties. GAO estimated the contract would result in annual savings of about $6 million. Furthermore, according to officials at Fort Gordon, the contractor's employees are providing better service than provided previously by federal employees.

Typically from 9 to 24 months is required for DOD to perform a cost comparison and take action on the results. In the case of Fort Gordon, it took five years. The three additional years of delay cost U.S. taxpayers $18 million, deprived the army of better service support, and kept 479 military personnel occupied with commercial functions rather than military duties. Sen. Sam Nunn of Georgia, a member of the Senate Armed Services Committee, is responsible in large part for this delay. According to a local union official, Nunn told the union "he threw up every roadblock he could" to contracting out.

One tactic that may delay contracting out while intimidating executive branch officials is for an individual congressman to request a GAO audit of the cost comparison studies, along with an investigation of allegations made by the threatened federal employees and their union. In nearly all instances the congressman is simply doing a favor for his constituents by requesting the audit or investigation, but it comes at significant expense to the taxpayers. Three examples:

- Rep. Tony P. Hall of Ohio, in August 1979, requested GAO to investigate an allegation that contracting out of laundry services at Wright-Patterson Air Force Base, Ohio, was not cost effective and had other undesirable effects. GAO determined that not only was the air force correct in determining that a cost savings would result, but that the air force estimate of $30,000 savings over three years was low. GAO increased the estimated savings to $387,000 and disposed of the other objections to the contract.

- Rep. Charles E. Bennett of Florida, in May 1980, requested GAO to review cost comparisons that resulted in the contracting out of vehicle maintenance and operations at the U.S. Naval Station, Mayport, Fla. GAO concluded that while use of a lower fringe benefit factor under former guidelines would not support the result, the use of a higher federal fringe benefit factor under then-current guidelines would result in estimated savings of $246,000 per year by contracting out.
- Rep. Doug Barnard, Jr. of Georgia, in May 1980, requested GAO to review the cost comparison study that resulted in contracting out installation support functions at Fort Gordon, Georgia, along with allegations made by the local union. GAO concluded that the contract would result in savings of about $5.7 million annually. GAO rejected the local union's allegations.

A chain of events describes what typically happens. Federal employees concerned about the possible loss of their high-paying federal jobs appeal to their congressional representatives. Then various organizations take up their cause with arguments concerning national security and other matters that are really smoke screens aimed at protecting and maintaining the federal jobs. Individual members of Congress respond by blocking or delaying the contracting of services; they employ such tactics as holding hearings or arranging for GAO audits and investigations. Congress as a body then enacts moratoriums, restrictions, and burdensome requirements for cost studies.

The executive branch at its upper levels in turn compromises on policy and waivers in its determination to proceed with implementation. OMB juggles federal costs in the cost comparisons to favor retaining federal employees, a politically popular result. Agencies react to a faltering policy direction by not identifying all the commercial functions they are performing, and by taking minimal action to contract out those functions as were known.

This chain of events has now tightened until the program to rely on the private sector for commercial services has almost suffocated. U.S. citizens each year are paying perhaps $5 billion more than necessary, and receiving poorer service in the bargain, by having their government in the business of providing commercial services. At this time perhaps only Congress has the means of loosening and breaking the chain.

V. Restoring The Balance of Power: Item Veto

When the federal budget is delivered to Capitol Hill in February of each year, it is viewed by the various committees of Congress as merely a starting point, a series of suggestions, which they may accept, reject, or revise.

If the administration wants to start a new program or continue one that is due to expire, the authorizing committee with jurisdiction must be persuaded to consider and adopt the necessary new legislation. At the same time the House and Senate budget committees, charged with viewing the overall federal budget against a broad background of economic performance and expectations, is taking its own measure of the administration's spending proposals.

After the president has submitted his budget, the appropriations subcommittees divide up the plan according to each one's area of jurisdiction. The House Appropriations Subcommittee on Transportation, for example, has charge of all spending for the Department of Transportation (DOT)—all of it. Over the eight months or so following submission of the department's budget, the secretary of transportation, along with the administrators of the various DOT agencies, will appear at hearings called by the subcommittee chairman, where they will explain and justify their spending requests.

Sometimes the DOT officials have to explain and justify why they want more money—although more often recently they have had to explain why they want less. For example the Urban Mass Transportation Administration (UMTA) has been trying to phase out operating subsidies to major metropolitan transit systems, on grounds that mass transit is primarily a local matter and that subsidies impede the development of realistic fare levels. But members of Congress, particularly those from locales with transit systems receiving these subsidies, have not allowed a phaseout. They simply put the money back into the budget. Beyond that, UMTA may or may not want to spend funds for a subway system in a particular city. Or the Federal Aviation Administration may want funds to expand an airport in one community, or close an airport tower in another.

Congress can require the agency to build a subway where it, not the agency, wants. Congress can keep a control tower open by voting the funds to operate it and inserting language in the reports that accompany the spending bills requiring the secretary of transportation to keep the tower open. The pressures on each member of Congress, then, run toward serving the interests of constituents, as well as those special interests with influence in the state or district, without concern for the impact of any individual spending decision on the nation as a whole.

A time-honored way in which Congress transmits this pressure to the executive branch is through the legislative "rider." This is language added onto a bill that has no direct bearing on the main thrust of the measure, and so merely rides along with it. The rules of both the House and Senate supposedly bar this practice, but they are often ignored. Congress uses such riders not only to impose spending directions and requirements on the executive branch but also to direct management operations and even override management decisions.

In May 1983, for example, the Farmers Home Administration, an agency within the Department of Agriculture, announced plans to move its Hawaii office from Hilo to Honolulu. The agency's appropriations bill did not specifically bar the move, which could have been done with language forbidding the expenditure of funds to pay for it. Rather, in reports that accompanied the spending measure, the House and Senate agricultural appropriations subcommittees both advised against it. The House report said that "The Committee does not feel this move is in the best interest of farmers and rural residents and directs Farmers Home to maintain the office in Hilo."

The agency responded that since the report language was not actual legislation, it was not legally binding, adding that the agency planned to proceed with the move. Brave, if not brash, words, for congressional reaction was swift. A supplemental appropriations bill was being considered about that time, and to it was added the following language: "None of the funds appropriated by this or any other Act may be used to relocate the Hawaii State office of the Farmers Home Administration from Hilo, Hawaii, to Honolulu, Hawaii." If the president believed that his Agriculture officials were right, and the Farmers Home Administration office should be moved, the only way he could back them up would be by vetoing that entire supplemental appropriations bill. That would have affected essential funding for the food stamp program and also for the departments of Commerce, Justice, State, Defense, and Health and Human Services, along with the Food and Drug Administration and numerous other agencies. In effect all were held hostage to that single 31-word sentence. Unless the president felt that the move of that office was a vital matter of national interest, he had no real option but to approve the entire bill—and thus prevent his administration executives from implementing a plan they believed would have improved operational efficiency.

Often enough Congress does not have to adopt actual legislation, as in the Farmers Home Administration case, to impose its will on the executive branch. Most agencies will follow committee report language because they know how easily it can find its way into law. Directives to spend, or not to spend, are not confined to legislation and committee reports; they may come at hearings, be in letters, or simply be in the form of a suggestion during a telephone call.

Congress controls not only the substance of legislation but also the timing for its consideration. The government's legal power to spend funds, and thus literally do anything, ends with the close of a fiscal year unless spending authority and appropriations have been enacted for the next fiscal year.

Thus Congress can essentially tie a president's hands—and it has done so, by sending him just before a fiscal year ends a multiagency spending bill that covers many different programs and includes requirements and prohibitions that were neither requested nor wanted by the administration, and perhaps were even opposed by it. Harry S Truman described this practice as a form of legislative blackmail, because the choice then became very simple: Swallow hard and sign the bill, or veto it and bring all the agencies and programs in it to a grinding halt. As a result, unless spending measures contain really serious problems for an administration, or force upon it policy decisions with which it fundamentally disagrees, presidents are more likely to sign bills they would rather have vetoed.

The Constitution requires that every bill passed by the House and Senate, shall, before it becomes law, be presented to the president either for signature if he approves or rejection if he disapproves. The framers of the Constitution in those days envisioned the term "bill" in a far narrower sense than it is used today. In the early days of the federal government, each bill was concerned with a single, specific subject, clearly identified in the title. In these circumstances a presidential veto affected only that subject and not any others. Since then, Congress has enlarged the number and scope of unrelated subjects lumped within a single "bill," until we have today omnibus appropriations bills and continuing resolutions that cover dozens of programs entailing billions of dollars. In these cases the president is effectively shorn of his ability to selectively veto bad legislation.

In effect the president is often not afforded a realistic opportunity to veto excessive spending bills because that power is empty when its use would bring the entire government, or a major portion of it, to a halt. In this manner one of the principal checks and balances in our system of government is effectively eliminated, and Congress knows it.

One way to remedy this problem, and to restore the badly eroded balance of power between the president and Congress, is to institute an item veto, such as is available to the governors of 43 states. Item veto power would enable a president to delete from major legislation such unrelated matters as the prohibition against moving the Farmers Home Administration office from Hilo to Honolulu without affecting the rest of the measure. Congress would still be able to exercise its constitutional right to override that veto, if it could.

While item veto authority first appeared among states of the Confederacy, it has spread rapidily since the Civil War period. Fourteen states had adopted it by 1882; by 1950 the total was up to 38 states. Today all but seven states (Indiana, Maine, Nevada, New Hampshire, North Carolina, Rhode Island, and Vermont) have conferred item veto authority on their governors.

Nor has Congress been afraid of the item veto, at least in principle, since it vested that authority in the territorial governors of Hawaii and Alaska in 1900 and 1912. The territorial governors of the Philippines, Puerto Rico, Guam, and the Virgin Islands also enjoyed this authority by virtue of congressional action.

In addition to its obvious support among state legislatures, item veto authority at the federal level has widespread support nationally. Such diverse groups as the League of Women Voters, the U.S. Chamber of Commerce, and the American Farm Bureau Federation have expressed support for the concept. So have liberal and conservative leaders in Congress from both major parties, such as Sen. Strom Thurmond, Sen. Hubert H. Humphrey, Sen. Everett M.

Dirksen, and Rep. Emanuel Celler. In 1979 a Gallup poll found that 70 percent of Americans favored giving the president item veto authority.

Opponents, such as House majority leader Jim Wright of Texas, claim the item veto would give a president "dictatorial powers," while the *Washington Post*, in October 1983, said in an editorial that it would enable a president to "terrorize Congress into going along on the most important matters."

Overlooked in these arguments is the very real fact that, given the current manner in which spending is legislated, with billions of dollars of programs lumped into a single bill that often includes a catchall title containing single paragraphs requiring or prohibiting spending on such unrelated matters as moving an agency office, the president's constitutional veto power is practically worthless. In addition the availability to a president of only a single political weapon, which can be used only in extremis, means that Congress has even wider latitude to meddle in agency affairs through language in committee reports. This language, often written by staff members and barely glanced at even by congressmen, attains the coercive value of law if an agency believes it risks legislation by ignoring it. Power is perception, and to the extent that an agency perceives that it must follow directives that are extralegal, then the finely wrought balance of power prescribed in the Constitution is nullified.

This problem has been exacerbated since the mid-1970s with the proliferation of subcommittees and staff that focus on ever narrower agendas, which their sponsoring congressmen use to "logroll" for support among themselves. Thus an agency can be tied up by the whim of a single member of Congress without even the review of a full committee, much less one body, and even less the enactment of legislation presented to a president.

Matters were made worse during this period by enactment of the Budget Control and Impoundment Act of 1974. This measure established the now familiar budget process in Congress, with the House and Senate budget committees and the Congressional Budget Office. Less closely noticed, however, were the provisions that eliminated a presidential practice going back at least as far as Thomas Jefferson, which had saved many a congressman from the consequences of his own fiscal folly.

Since Jefferson was the nation's chief executive, presidents had asserted the right to "impound"—simply not spend—appropriated monies if they thought it in the best national interest to do so. No one had challenged this practice; neither was it conducted in a high-profile manner. As a result Congress, the executive branch, and the taxpayers all benefited: the congressman, by trumpeting passage of a favored spending bill; the president by simply not spending the funds, thereby helping to retain some semblance of fiscal sanity; and of course the taxpayer.

The 1974 Budget Act ended all this by formalizing the principle that all funds appropriated by Congress *must* be spent. If the president wishes not to do so, he must inform Congress through a regular process in which Congress has the last word, either by agreeing to delete the spending or by insisting on it.

In the ten years preceding adoption of the Budget Act, federal spending grew by $151 billion, from $118.6 billion in 1964 to $269.6 billion in 1974. In the ten years following, it grew another $620 billion, or more than four times the pace of the previous decade. Whatever brakes on spending existed before the inaptly named Budget Act was passed have since been taken off, and remain off, as the federal budget approaches the $900 billion mark and the national debt exceeds $1.3 trillion.

Whether Congress ever will face up to its responsibilities in this mess is doubtful. Sen. Mack Mattingly of Georgia and Sen. Alan J. Dixon of Illinois have both introduced legislation providing for an item veto, but the only formal Senate action taken thus far has been a resounding rejection of Mattingly's proposal.

Mattingly sought to establish an item veto through legislation, attaching his measure as an amendment to legislation on boat safety. It was defeated 65-34, but some senators, including majority leader Howard Baker, who voted against the Mattingly proposal said they did so because they preferred a constitutional approach.

Dixon has introduced a resolution calling for a constitutional amendment to provide for a line item veto, thus protecting it from the vagaries of individual Congresses. (The argument against the Mattingly approach was that what one Congress might give a president, a subsequent one could take away, assuming of course it had the votes to override an expected presidential veto.) The Senate Judiciary Subcommittee on the Constitution had held one hearing on Dixon's proposal as of June 1984.

John Marshall, the nation's first Chief Justice, once wrote that "it is the peculiar province of the legislature to prescribe general rules for the government of society; the application of those rules would seem to be the duty of other departments."

The virtue of item veto authority is that it does not require Congress to reform its nature. While enabling the executive to curb congressional excesses, Congress would retain the ultimate legislative authority through its power to override a veto. Even so such a tool would help considerably to reduce the proliferation of congressional encroachments that now threaten to choke the executive branch's ability to manage the operations of the federal government.

Other Recommendations

Military Base Realignment

A bipartisan council of defense experts should be convened to examine the national military base structure and recommend closings and consolidations without consideration to parochial interests or pressures.

Government Printing Office

The president should request Congress to establish wage parity for Government Printing Office employees in line with the pay scales of other federal workers.

The president should seek to strengthen the role of the public printer to enable him to take charge and manage the agency free of congressional micromanaging.

Commissaries

Commissaries operating in metropolitan areas in violation of statutory authority should be closed or consolidated, while the subsidy to all others should be reduced to lower the cost burden to American taxpayers.

Contracting Out

The president should request that Congress endorse the principle of agencies' contracting out as set forth in OMB Circular A-76.

The executive branch should conduct a governmentwide study by function for the purpose of contracting out.

An appeals process and review board should be established within the executive branch to monitor A-76 actions to ensure that proper steps are taken to protect the rights of affected federal employees.

Reporting Requirements

The president should seek a Sunset Reporting Requirements Act, which would provide that all current requirements will expire in two years and that all future recurring requirements will expire two years after enactment.

Budget Process

The president should request that Congress go to a biannual system of budgeting and appropriations in which the first year of a Congress, or the odd-numbered year, is taken up with oversight and review, while the actual appropriations legislation is considered during the second, or even-numbered, year.

About the Authors

Randall Fitzgerald is a former reporter for columnist Jack Anderson, and covered Congress for newspapers in seven states as a reporter for Capitol Hill News Service. He now writes frequently on public policy issues for *Reader's Digest*, the *Wall Street Journal*, and other publications. He is the author of two previous books.

Gerald Lipson, an award-winning newspaper reporter currently in the Washington bureau of the *New York Post*, has also written for the *Chicago Daily News*, the *Washington Star*, the *Wilmington News-Journal*, and United Press International.

His congressional credits include service as press secretary to House Minority Leader John J. Rhodes, Senator Charles H. Percy, and Rep. John B. Anderson, and as minority spokesman for the House Budget Committee. A graduate of Northwestern University's Medill School of Journalism, he lives with his wife and family in Bethesda, Md.

Cato Institute

Founded in 1977, the Cato Institute is a public policy research foundation dedicated to broadening the parameters of policy debate to allow consideration of more options that are consistent with the traditional American principles of limited government, individual liberty, and peace. Toward that goal, the Institute strives to achieve a greater involvement of the intelligent, concerned lay public in questions of policy and the proper role of government.

The Institute is named for *Cato's Letters,* pamphlets that were widely read in the American Colonies in the early eighteenth century and played a major role in laying the philosophical foundation for the revolution that followed. Since that revolution, civil and economic liberties have been eroded as the number and complexity of social problems have grown. Today virtually no aspect of human life is free from the domination of a governing class of politico-economic interests. A pervasive intolerance for individual rights is shown by government's arbitrary intrusions into private economic transactions and its disregard for civil liberties.

To counter this trend the Cato Institute undertakes an extensive publications program dealing with the complete spectrum of policy issues. Books, monographs, and shorter studies are commissioned to examine the federal budget, social security, regulation, NATO, international trade, and a myriad of other issues. Major policy conferences are held throughout the year from which papers are published thrice yearly in the *Cato Journal.*

In order to maintain an independent posture, the Cato Institute accepts no government funding. Contributions are received from foundations, corporations, and individuals, and other revenue is generated from the sale of publications. The Institute is a non-profit, tax-exempt, educational foundation under Section 501(c)3 of the Internal Revenue Code.

CATO INSTITUTE
224 Second St., S.E.
Washington, D.C. 20003